# GROWING UP
# TORRES
# STRAIT
# ISLANDER
## IN AUSTRALIA

ABORIGINAL AND TORRES STRAIT ISLANDER
READERS ARE ADVISED THAT THIS BOOK CONTAINS
WRITING BY, AND NAMES AND IMAGES OF,
DECEASED PERSONS.

# GROWING UP
# TORRES STRAIT ISLANDER
## IN AUSTRALIA

## EDITED BY
# SAMANTHA FAULKNER

Published by Black Inc.,
an imprint of Schwartz Books Pty Ltd
Wurundjeri Country
22–24 Northumberland Street
Collingwood VIC 3066, Australia
enquiries@blackincbooks.com
www.blackincbooks.com

9781760644420 (paperback)
9781743823552 (ebook)

 A catalogue record for this
book is available from the
NATIONAL
LIBRARY National Library of Australia
OF AUSTRALIA

Cover design by Beau Lowenstern
Text design by Tristan Main
Typesetting by Beau Lowenstern
Back cover: Torres Strait Islander Flag designed by Bernard Namok
Reproduced by permission of the Torres Strait Island Regional Council
Map by Alan Laver

pp. 17–33: Edited and abridged extract from *Edward Koiki Mabo: His Life and
Struggle for Land Rights* © Noel Loos and Eddie Koiki Mabo 1996; first published
by University of Queensland Press, Brisbane. Reproduced by permission of the
Mabo family and the publisher.
pp. 73–74: 'Matriarch' © Jillian Boyd-Bowie 2021; first published in *Borderless:
A Transnational Anthology of Feminist Poetry*, Recent Work Press, Canberra.
Reproduced by permission of the author.
pp. 121–126: Extract from 'The Learning Time', *Somebody Now: The
Autobiography of Ellie Gaffney, a Woman of Torres Strait* © Ellie Gaffney 1989; first
published by Aboriginal Studies Press, Canberra. Reproduced by permission of
Maryann Ansey.
pp. 127–141: Extract from *Eded Mer (My Life)* © Thomas Lowah 1988; first
published by The Rams Skull Press, Kuranda. Reproduced by permission of
Neari Vanhooren.
pp. 142–152: Extract from *Ina's Story: The Memoir of a Torres
Strait Islander Woman* © Catherine Titasey 2011. Reproduced by permission of
the author and Copyright Agency Australia.

# Contents

*A Note on Spelling*

Some words, place names and expressions have multiple valid spellings. In this book, we have opted to use the spelling that is most authentic to the authors or primary sources.

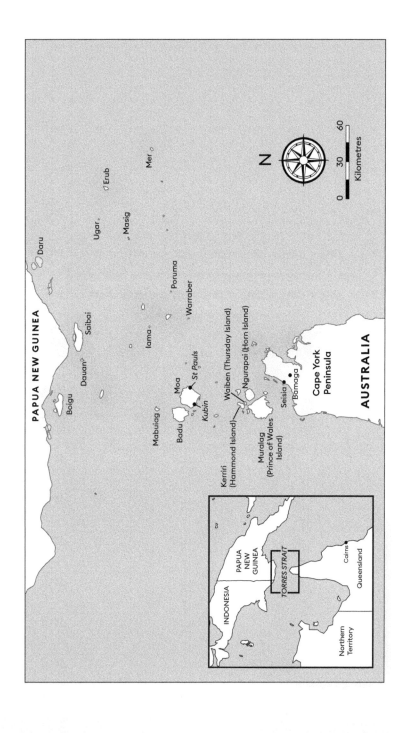

# Introduction

## Samantha Faulkner

One of my earliest memories was going out fishing for the day with my family. I would be woken, along with my sisters, by Mum when it was still dark. We would get dressed and have a quick cup of tea and maybe some toast. We would set off as early as we could in the morning, or as early as my sisters and I could manage to get up. Everyone would carry something – food, water, petrol, fishing equipment – from home down the hill to the dinghy.

The dinghy was loaded up with supplies, safely stored in hidden, neat compartments, tucked away so they would not get in anyone's way. Everyone would jump on board and we would push off to our destination. Grandad would fire up the outboard motor and then we were off. The smell of the fresh salty air and the wind in my hair filled me with expectation, joy and excitement.

I loved the days when the water was calm. Grandad would call it a neap tide. We would leave Thursday Island behind and either head to one of Grandad's secret fishing spots or look for orchids or go for a swim on a nearby island or collect oysters and birds' eggs. There were a lot of choices and many adventures to be had.

One day we arrived at a yellow, sandy beach. My sisters jumped off the dinghy into the water and walked to the shore. Nana and Grandad also jumped into the water, and the sand moved around them. It was a small shark swimming in the shallow water.

'Come on,' they yelled.

'No, shark,' I replied and pointed to it.

I thought it might bite me. I was too scared to jump in the water. I did not want to leave the safety of the dinghy.

Grandad waded back through the water to the dinghy and lifted me up in his arms. He carried me to the beach. I held on to him but also turned my head to look down and keep an eye on the shark swimming beneath me. He plonked me down on the shore. I was safe.

I can still see him now. He was a tall man. That day he wore shorts and a T-shirt with a wide-brimmed straw hat. He was a calm, no-nonsense man.

This is just one of the memories I have of growing up in the Torres Strait. My childhood was filled with fishing, playing, eating and school. My playmates were my sisters and school friends. Looking back on it now, it was a good time and one that I cherish.

*

The Torres Strait is the most northerly part of Australia. It is a group of islands south of Papua New Guinea and north of Cape York Peninsula, Queensland. It is made up of five community groups: Northern (Boigu, Dauan, Saibai); Eastern (Erub, Mer, Ugar); Western (St Pauls, Kubin, Badu, Mabuiag); Central (Masig, Poruma, Warraber, Iama); Southern (Waiben/ Thursday, Horn, Prince of Wales and Hammond, the northern peninsula area and mainland Australia).

The island groupings are best represented on the Torres Strait Islander flag, designed by the late Bernard Namok. The five-pointed star represents the five groups and also symbolises navigation, as Torres Strait Islander people are a seafaring people. The white star symbolises peace, too.

The Torres Strait Islander flag was adopted in 1992. It symbolises the unity and identity of Torres Strait Islanders. The white Dhari is a headdress and some say it signifies our culture. The colour green is for the land, black is for the people and blue is for the sea.

The Torres Strait Islander population is about 70,000, with the majority of that number living on mainland Australia. In the 2021 Australian Bureau of Statistics Census, there were 69,848 people who identified as being of Torres Strait Islander descent (33,765 were Torres Strait Islander and 36,083 identified as both Aboriginal and Torres Strait Islander). The total Aboriginal and/or Torres Strait Islander population was 812,728, or 3.2 per cent of the population. 742,882 people (2.9 per cent) identified as Aboriginal.

*

Identity and representation are important to Torres Strait Islanders.

Most Australians have heard of Eddie Koiki Mabo, who in 1992, along with the other plaintiffs (Salee, Mapo, Rice and

Passi), refuted the myth of terra nullius and had their traditional lands recognised by the High Court of Australia. This was a landmark decision which led to recognition of Aboriginal and Torres Strait Islander peoples' ongoing and continuing links to country. Mabo Day is celebrated on 3 June each year and is a recognised Bank Holiday in the Torres Strait.

Many years later, in 2018, the then governor-general of Australia, His Excellency General the Honourable Sir Peter Cosgrove AK MC and his wife, Lady Cosgrove, travelled to Mer Island. It was an historic occasion and a big event for the small community. They were welcomed at a traditional ceremony as guests of Mr Aven Noah, Member for Mer, Torres Strait Regional Authority. Then, their Excellencies laid a wreath at the grave of Eddie Koiki Mabo, as guests of Mr Alo Tapim, a Senior Elder of the Mer Island community, and suggested other leaders do the same.

'Eddie Mabo inspires us all,' said Sir Cosgrove in a speech to the Meriam people. 'He lies here for eternity, but his memory and his example will be an example to all Australians, First Australians and the rest of us, for time into the future, so it's a privilege for Lyn and I to be here. We follow in the footsteps of prime ministers, previous governors-general. Let it be said, it might become – perhaps should become – a rite of passage, a necessary journey by every future prime minister, by every future governor-general.' I would have to agree.

Travel to Mer Island starts with a flight from Cairns to Horn Island. The flight is about one and a half to two hours. A charter plane from Horn Island to Mer then takes another one to two hours. The views take your breath away, as does the landing on the short airstrip. Permission to visit from the Island Council must be obtained beforehand. Visitors need to arrange to be met at the airport and taken to the gravesite, and also need to arrange accommodation for the night. It is not a spur-of-the-moment decision.

A trip in 2023 to Thursday Island with family was insightful and emotional. My family members reminisced about their own growing up many years before. I walked the path I used to take to school and church, retracing those footsteps from an older and hopefully wiser point of view.

What has changed? What has remained the same? Well, there are more crocodiles. More tourists in town, which is good for business. It was great to be embraced by the heat and by friends who have returned up north to live. The wongai fruit was just about ready to eat. Hibiscus and frangipani were blooming. Everything looked green.

The prices were still high at IBIS, the local supermarket, especially for fruit and vegetables. Part of this is to account for the high transport and shipping costs. The local bakery was up for sale for $1.5 million.

I took a dinghy to Friday Island to visit Kazu Pearl Farm. On the water again. The colours changing from green to blue and back again. Looking to the horizon to see the outline of distant islands. Scanning the shorelines for turtle tracks or crocodile tracks or just crocodiles in general.

A few lucky ones in the dinghy saw a turtle come up for air. Small fish were jumping out of the water too. The smell of salt water was welcoming. It permeated my whole being. The salt water spray too. And the smell of coral was something else – could it be the truffle of the sea?

The wind was strong crossing the open channel, but as we took shelter close to the islands it died down a bit. We travelled slowly, and it was a lovely cruise around Waiben (Thursday)

Island, Kiriri (Hammond) Island, Goods Island, Friday Island and Muralag (Prince of Wales) Island.

Which leads me to the themes of this book. These essays are important. Each one is unique and beautiful. The broad themes focus on family, identity and representation. There is wisdom, lessons to learn, encouragement, love, culture, and connection with other cultures. A number of contributors discuss what it is like to live in two or more worlds. This is a common and shared theme with Aboriginal Australians also.

The writers are honest and trust us with their stories – stories that have shaped who they are today. Some of this history is raw and resilient. There is humour, too, another theme shared with Aboriginal Australians. Humour provides us with strength and a common bond, which provides a base from which to be resilient.

The four excerpts (by Thomas Lowah, Edward Koiki Mabo, Ellie Gaffney and Ina Titasey, née Mills) honour Elders who have gone before us. They describe what life was like in a different time. This provides a great contrast with the other stories in the following pages.

I hope that you enjoy all the stories and are spurred on to visit the Torres Strait.

Thanks to Black Inc. for saying yes to a *Growing Up Torres Strait Islander in Australia* anthology, and thanks to the contributors for trusting their stories to this publication.

Eso, Kaima Eso, Au Eso Au!

Samantha Faulkner
*Editor*

## *Coconut-Oil Chronicles*

### Lenora Thaker

'You got to make that coconut talk!' my father would growl. By talk, he meant the sound the coconut should make when you were scraping out its hard but sweet and tasty white meat on the madu.*

Scraping coconut on the sharp teeth of a madu was definitely an art and a skill to be practised if you didn't want the fluffy shredded coconut meat it produced turning from white to red, and if you didn't want to wear BandAids for a week.

It was the 1970s when we dared suggest to Dad that there was probably a labour-saving home appliance that could do the job. After all, Mum had a Mixmaster for baking, so we didn't have to spend time and energy slaving over hand beaters anymore. But Dad would not be persuaded.

'It won't give you that proper fine coconut!' he would argue. For him, this was serious business. Longstanding traditions and proven methods, handed down from generation to generation, would not be tampered with. So that was the end of that.

I remember our original madu. It was so old. It must have travelled with the ancestors on that first voyage from the Islands to the mainland in the 1920s. The metal piece was the colour of rust, and thinking back now, I wonder if that added to the flavour of our dishes. That and the sweat that would pour off Dad when he was in full coconut-scraping flight.

The wood of the madu had the look and texture of a hundred-year-old railway sleeper. Maybe it was once part of the decking of an old pearling lugger? Or a piece of discarded picket fencing from the home of the London Missionary Society missionaries? Who knows – upcycling was a way of life in those days.

Our grandma was an expert on the madu and could scrape as good as the men. But for me, it was the most uncomfortable piece of equipment to use, that's for sure. I remember using one of Grandma's old embroidered cushions for added comfort. Unfortunately, it was my undoing, for I could neither balance properly nor make that coconut 'talk'.

I think Dad wanted me to be a champion on the madu. We'd be under the house and he'd be barking instructions.

Then Mum would yell from upstairs: 'Get her off that thing! Bambai we'll be up the hospital all night when she cuts herself!'

Luckily for me it never came to that. It was one of the first and last occasions I got to drive the old madu. But with our insatiable demand for coconut oil, sop sop or sabi fish and rice, Dad barely had time to let the madu rest.

\*

Coconut oil was a health and beauty staple in almost every Ailan family's home, including ours. Most of my childhood, up until at least the age of twelve, was spent sitting babook (cross-legged) at the feet of my grandmothers, having my long hair coconut-oiled, combed and braided. My mother wouldn't let us go catch the bus for school unless we were lathered in oil from head to toe. It was as if our chalky arms and legs might be mistaken for child neglect, so we couldn't leave the house unless we were glistening. Boys would be checked for adequate coconut oil coverage on their way out the door to their footy game. It would be better not to come home if a match was lost because a bala couldn't slip out of a tackle.

'It's your secret weapon … make you fly down that field and no one can catch you,' the grandmas would gleefully say, as though the coconut oil their hard-work made possessed some mystical qualities.

But to be dipped in coconut oil every day before school wasn't without its drawbacks. I remember sitting in class one day in the late 1960s. Our desks were so old, they still had holes for inkpots. When I stood up, the little white boy sitting next to me noticed two oily patches on the wooden bench where the backs of my thighs had rested.

'What's that?!' he said, loud enough to attract attention and pointing to where I'd sat. Then, '*Eeeyew* … what's that smell?!' he said, holding his nose as though he'd gotten the whiff of a passing dunny cart.

If anything, I smelled rather pleasantly like an Anzac biscuit. So this was a complete overreaction from a pretender and a bully, I thought. Anyway, I was that embarrassed, I wanted to punch that boy. But when you're the only black kid in the classroom, you have to pick and choose your battles. So I quickly rubbed the seat with my hand, blending and giving it a nice, even shine. With the evidence more or less erased, I pretended not to know what this boy was on about. One thing I did after that, though, was take over from my mother the job of very lightly applying my own coconut oil in the mornings. But it didn't help. That lovingly homemade moisturiser and cure-all was too good. So by the end of that school year my seat was the nicest, most polished of timber grain to be had.

*

The grandmas have long passed now, and, recently, so has our champion coconut husker and scraper, Dad. Mum has long retired from coconut-oil making and I never took up this labour-intensive tradition. But wonderfully, nowadays we can order our coconut oil online from a Torres Strait Islander business that produces amazing coconut-oil products locally.

A pretty 200 millilitre bottle sits on my vanity. Some days I just like to unscrew the lid, put the bottle under my nose and draw up the rich, nutty coconut scent. It instantly transports me back to those childhood days, being amongst our old people, learning how to live in the world, and, most important, knowing what it is to be growing up Torres Strait Islander.

---

\* A madu is basically a thin plank of wood, no more than a yard long in the old measurement, with a flat metal piece with sharp, tooth-like grooves fixed to one end of the plank. The user straddles the instrument over a chair or stool, as you would if you were, say, riding a horse or a bike. Then you cup the husked half-coconut between your hands and use fairly rapid forward movements to shred the insides over the madu's teeth.

# *Together, Our Differences Make Us Strong*

## Thomas Mayo

As a boy, being a Torres Strait Islander was simply about being different – an Islander living on Larrakia Land in the tropical capital city of the Northern Territory, Darwin. At the school I went to, there were no other Torres Strait Islander children. None of the other children had delicious powna (the thick, tough outer skin of the dugong that when boiled for long enough becomes soft and delicious) and soy sauce wrapped in cling wrap or tasty leftover turtle-steak sandwiches for lunch. I was the only kid who could brag about going hunting at sea. I was the only one who had tight curly hair – too tight to make spikey like my straight-haired friends.

I was a shy boy. Dancing at a school disco was a stretch too far. I was taller than the others, as skinny as a skeleton and feeling as awkward as I looked. Yet when it came to island dancing or playing rugby with my cousins, I was at my happiest. I could perform in front of a hundred people at a ceremony such as a wedding or tombstone unveiling; I was a leader on the field.

There was something about the voices of my Elders lifting in a powerful harmony – the reverberating warup (drum) and the rattle of the kulap (handheld rattle), emphasising my pride and the vigour in my step; I relished the work on the field, fighting hard to win as a warrior would.

As a teenager, when the Torres Strait Islander flag was created by Bernard Namok Snr, my pride in being an Islander gained colour – black, green, white and blue. Being an Islander also gained a popular contemporary sound. For the first time, I heard my language and culture expressed in a way that other young people could sing and dance along with too – Christine Anu was a pop icon for youth in my day. She helped put the Torres Strait on the map.

After Year 12, I applied for two traineeships. One as an electrician with the Power and Water Authority and the other as a maritime trainee at the Port Authority. When I got the call from the Port Authority to offer me the job, I was sure the interviewers were moved by my strong desire to work close to the sea.

I loved working at the port. Throughout two years of doing a little of everything – from delivering post to doing security and guarding the port gates; from being a shipping agent, servicing the ships to being a deckhand on pilot boats – I gained an intimate understanding of the maritime industry, including the characters and politics in workplaces.

My favourite work was on the wharves, in the role of a stevedore, loading and unloading cargo from ships. I loved learning to drive the massive forklifts and cranes, and after the traineeship, I continued in the occupation for sixteen years.

Being a wharfie had its perks. At smoko breaks, or while waiting for cargo or a ship, I would climb down the large rocks on the edge of the wharf to fish with a light line and small pieces of bait. I'd catch mostly bream, greasy rock cod and golden snapper for dinner. If I felt like eating mullet, I would fetch my long bamboo spear, which I'd secreted in some empty pipework beneath the wharf. On the rocks at the water's edge, I would stand as still as a brolga, and when a large mullet unwittingly swam by I'd strike.

Crabs were on the menu too. Setting pots flat on the mud at low tide produced the best results. Before work, I baited the pots. As I approached the wharf apron, I laid them down. At the end of my shift, I retrieved them, often with a few big mud crabs, on the way past. Crab spring rolls, chilli crab, curry crab, steamed crab with ginger and spring onions – I caught so many crabs in those days, I had to learn many different ways to cook them, for variety.

'Are you going fishing, Dad?' the kids would ask me, when I put on my work boots and uniform.

My dad was an Island man of his time, one of many who left the islands in the '60s and '70s to find work on the mainland. He was hard – both in his work ethic and his expectations that us kids would do well. I was told that my dad was harder than most. Perhaps this is why I was quietly spoken.

I found my voice thanks to my fellow wharfies. We had a strong union, the Maritime Union of Australia (MUA), that had long fought for our rights. They say 'a union is only as strong as its members'. How true that is. I saw it in practice.

In 1998, Prime Minister John Howard, who didn't like unions – I think he wasn't one for fairness at all – colluded with my employer, Patrick Stevedores, to try to destroy my union. I remember that for many months, Howard and much of the media had been reporting that wharfies like me were lazy and our workplace was rife with criminal activity. I knew these allegations weren't true.

On the morning of 8 April 1998, I was driving to work and listening to the radio. I heard that in the middle of the night, government and company-backed mercenaries had moved onto the wharves, in a military-like insurrection, physically dragging my co-workers through the gates and locking us out. I learnt that this was what all the negative media had been about. Howard and his co-conspirators were softening up the Australian public in order to brutally sack us.

I wondered, then, with a little family – me, my partner and two babies – if I had lost a well-paying job that I loved.

There were many reasons I became proud to be a wharfie and a member of the MUA. Not only did we use our strength as a union in a vital part of the logistics chain for our own benefit – the good rosters, wages and conditions – but we had often stood up and sacrificed for causes beyond our own – for social justice and the most vulnerable in society, both in Australia and abroad.

For my own people, the Indigenous people of Australia, the MUA was ahead of its time in acts of solidarity for First Nations justice. Seafarers and wharfies took action to support Aboriginal pastoral workers during the Pilbara Strike in 1946; they supported Yolngu people as they tried to protect Country with the Yirrkala Bark Petitions in 1963; wharfies took supplies to the striking Gurindji workers during the Gurindji Wave Hill Walk-Off that began in 1966; the union was an active campaigner for the 1967 referendum so that Indigenous people could be counted as Australia citizens; and the union office in Darwin printed pamphlets in support of the 1972 Larrakia petition for land rights.

When I learnt that wharfies raised money to help build a bakery on Moa Island in the '60s, to help overcome the negligence of the state, and that Koiki Mabo was a union leader himself and had great support from the labour movement, how could I not be proud to be a wharfie, a union member and eventually an elected official?

In our time of crisis as wharfies during the 1998 Patricks lockout, these past actions in solidarity were paid back in kind. Much of the broader community joined the locked-out workers on the picket lines. With arms linked together, the community helped us to defy the sackings. With unity, a month later, we won.

I eventually became an elected leader of the MUA. I had learnt how to negotiate and build power, or how to leverage it. It was as a union delegate and official that I learnt to write and communicate effectively, to rouse up support and persuade fellow workers or move the boss.

I took what I learnt on the wharf and have applied those skills to furthering my own people's rights and interests. After helping to create the historic *Uluru Statement from the Heart* in late May 2017, I travelled with the sacred document to all parts of the continent, helping to build a people's movement, calling for its proposals for Voice, Treaty, Truth.

Once a shy Island boy, I have found myself as a national advocate for Indigenous rights and an author of six books, written in only four years, from 2019 to 2023. Each of the books has been written with a specific purpose – to help readers to understand the truth of our past and present, so that they will be motivated to right the wrongs against Aboriginal and Torres Strait Islander peoples. To give us a Voice.

My first book, *Finding the Heart of the Nation*, tells the story of the *Uluru Statement from the Heart*, and my follow-up book,

*Finding Our Heart*, does the same for children. *Freedom Day: The Story of Vincent Lingiari and the Wave Hill Walk-Off*, co-authored with Lingiari's granddaughter Rosie Smiler, shares the history of the walk-off and explains why Gurindji people supported the Voice referendum. *Dear Son*, my proudest work, is a deeply personal collection of letters from First Nations fathers and sons. I wrote to my eldest son and my father in that book – a healing process that I hope many will learn from.

I am following in my forebears' footsteps. Torres Strait Islanders were the first to build an Indigenous Voice – a representative body – following the 1936 Maritime Strike, in which pearling workers fought for better pay and conditions, and for island autonomy. Torres Strait Islanders defended our country, and as part of the defence force were paid less than the white soldiers. Those Elders too went on strike to fight for fairness. Torres Strait Islanders were part of the national leadership that led to all Indigenous people being counted when the 1967 referendum successfully removed discrimination from the constitution. All young Torres Strait Islanders should learn our proud history of standing up for our rights. And all Australians should too.

I'm still growing up as a Torres Strait Islander. My Elders gave me dance – the ability to move like a proud Torres Strait Islander. Athe Bernard Namok gave me colour – a flag to wear with pride. Deadly artists like Christine Anu and Mau Power provide subsequent generations of youth new ways to express our identity, while scholars of Torres Strait Island customs like Alick Tipoti keep the old ways alive.

Growing up Torres Strait Islander is being different. But together, our differences make us strong.

## *Edward Koiki Mabo: His Life and Struggle for Land Rights*

**Noel Loos and Eddie Koiki Mabo**

### WHO WAS THAT BOY

I knew him as a child of Islander birth, at home
on a beautiful island, the jewel of the Coral Sea
Frolicking on beaches and *op magerr* he loved to roam
or mastering – the art of *sisi* on the tallest coconut tree

### Who was that boy

*Apek kebile* for all his tender years
Trekking the miles to school was always a familiar sight
Of *lamar* and *lug-le* he boasted no fears
The *zogo* of his *arerr* he trusted and clinged to with might

## Who was that boy

Some ventured that David was his name
Others were in doubt as it was spelt with 'K'
Pebble however small has traded them both to fame
Dearly though the price that he had to pay

## Who was that boy

*Waitai* piped tunes by an ancient flute
*Maiso*'s zephyred strain a lullaby gentle and sweet
Twittering *toli* a faithful company *em-oot*
Are sure memories of *apek kebile*'s retreat

## Who was that boy

His name and memory will forever stand
Ranks with the greatest in the annals of our country
He did us all proud the indigenous of this land
Having knocked out *terra nullius* and now our land is free

## He was that boy

by Eidi Papa (George Mye)

Dedicated to the memory of a great Torres Strait Islander Australian, the son of a dinky-di *puar amissir-amissir* Meriam of the native title homeland – Mer Island in the Torres Strait.

**Glossary to 'Who Was That Boy'**

This poem was delivered by the late Commissioner George Mye MBE at a United Nations Working Group on Indigenous Populations in Geneva, Switzerland, in July 1995.

*op magerr*: area of garden land above the beaches leading up to the hills.

*sisi*: walking up a coconut tree with hands and legs goanna-style not frog-style.

*apek kebile*: the little boy from the far side of the island (*apek*: the other side, *kebile*: a small boy).

*lamar*: ghost, spirit. It could also refer to Europeans because of their pale skins.

*lug-le*: sorcerer (the greatest fear of Islanders even today).

*zogo*: sacred power.

*arerr*: ancestors.

*waitai*: the music created by the wind on bamboo fences erected as windbreaks.

*maiso*: the constant roar or rumbling of the waves on the nearby Great Barrier Reef; sound of the surf.

*toli*: small brown birds, 'sandpipers'.

*em-oot* (more usually *oot-em*): for sleep; while you sleep.

*puar*: vine.

*puar amissir-amissir*: a vine climbing round and round up a coconut tree. It is totemically significant, especially to Koiki Mabo's Piadram clan at Las.

\*

**Eddie Koiki Mabo**: I was born on Murray Island in 1936, and I was brought up by my uncle who then assigned me under his name when I first went to school. After I realised that I wasn't a Mabo, I didn't want to change because they were the only people that I knew in my early life and it was also an advantage for me to grow under that name because all the rest of my relatives were Sambos and there were too many of them, and there were too many to share the small bit of land that we had. And my adoptive parents told me that it would be better for me to stay because traditionally I became the head of the Mabos. And because of these things that I've learnt to realise the importance of, I then continued to be Mabo. I have no intention of changing my name back to Sambo because of these ideas that have been set in my mind by my parents.

Anyhow, I went to school on Murray and my first schoolteacher was Bakoi Baud. She was my infant teacher and she taught me in both Miriam Mir and in English, although her English wasn't as good; but nevertheless she made an attempt to try and teach me to understand the outside world through that language. She taught me to count and we used shells that we collected on the beach. That's how I learnt to count. As I grew up Sam Passi took over then, and my uncle, Meb Salee. Sam Passi was a teacher during the war years and Meb Salee joined him after the war and it was during that time that my uncle, Meb Salee, insisted that we speak English at all times in school, and I used to get into a lot of trouble over that because whatever Bakoi had taught me in the first place wasn't good enough for me to make conversation with others, so it was wrong for them to stop me from talking my language. But that didn't make any difference to me at all, because despite the fact that they used to belt me every time I talked Miriam, I continued to do so. And nearly every day I used to bend over the table for the old fellow, like Meb Salee, to give me a few straps on my backside.

Anyhow, after Meb Salee, although Meb Salee was still there, we had a white teacher by the name of Mr Cooley. Cooley, regardless of how smart he was, didn't make any difference to my education at all because I didn't understand him and he didn't understand me. And the same went for all the kids that were in school with me; and the only people that we were able to communicate with were the Island teachers. And he was only there to fill in time, to spend the Commonwealth or State money, whatever it was. After a while Mr Cooley left and we had a fellow by the name of Garlick, although we didn't know his first name. I never ever learnt their first names at all. Maybe in some ways we were forbidden to know his first name. I don't know why, but maybe as a kind of respect. Maybe.

After Mr Garlick, we had a very good teacher and a friend of all the schoolkids. His name was Robert Victor Miles. He came from Victoria. He completed his education degree in Melbourne University and he took a job during the war as an education officer, and then after a while he went up to the Straits and was an education officer of the Torres Strait Light Infantry Battalion. Then after that, he came home to Melbourne, that is, after the war, and applied for a job on TI (Thursday Island). Of course there were no jobs around the place, so they gave him a job as an administrative officer. I don't know what position he occupied, but he was in the office for a while. Then the vacancy came on Saibai. he went to Saibai and then later he came to Murray.

That was the biggest breakthrough that I have ever had in terms of the English language. He was the one that taught me the most of English language. He taught me to make conversation effectively with other people and he was there continuously for me to talk to him; and whenever I made a mistake, of course, he stopped me and explained the meaning of the word in my language. That was the advantage. He spoke fluent Miriam. The same thing happened on Saibai. He was a fluent Saibai speaker and he was the first teacher that told us not to stop using our language. And I continued to talk to him. He later asked me why I came to stay at his place when my mother and father went to TI. And I told him that he was the one that requested my stay there, requested me to come and stay. And he wanted to know the reason why I accepted it, and I said, 'Because there was no problem in communicating, and I wanted to practise to talk English language.' And he had me do it. It was a good exercise for him to have somebody, after school hours, to talk Miriam Mir as well, because it was an ideal situation for us, to exchange conversation in two languages; and I think I became the first Meriam man to speak so fluently. Not that I'm very good, but it's better than the majority of my people in that age group.

My lifetime on Murray, I think, was the best time of my life I ever spent, growing up on Murray and having an opportunity to learn both the whiteman way of life from my schoolteacher Robert Miles, and my traditional heritage as well.

*

When I was a kid growing up, one of the things that my uncle taught me was to make dugouts out of wood. I was really young then.

We rigged the dugout canoe up fully the way they used to have it, the traditional sailing canoe. And we used to go out fishing, mainly around the home reef on Murray. Then after a while he'd pull the sails down and we just used to paddle, paddle out with outriggers on it. That was during the war years. My mother used to use it a lot. She used to go out after what they call rock cods. At a certain time of the year the rock cod comes out on Murray in abundance. Got some reef fish to eat too. We ceased to use the dugout canoe, but that was the only training I had. Actually I picked navigation up from my dad when occasionally he would work on the dinghies, sailing dinghies. And I'd go out with him for a day or two, and I got used to sailing, sailing with just a sail boat, no motor on it. And then when I came to TI, then all they did was to teach us to read compasses with north, south, east and west, and how to read charts, how to get from one reef to the other. That was the only thing they taught us and for radio things, mainly to turn it on and turn to the frequency, or whatever, and just listen to it and how to press the thing before you talk. That was the only thing they taught us.

*

**Noel Loos**: What made you think that the education you were getting was not a good one?

**Eddie Koiki Mabo**: Well, I actually experienced it myself when I came to TI. See Blacks were segregated in one school at a place called Ling's Camp and the other school was situated for the Whites on the Green Hills.

I was told that the white school had offered much more in terms of the study of science, for instance. There was more taught in social studies; there was more taught in geography and all that kind of stuff. There was nothing like that happening to us. All we were learning was to read and write. We didn't even study our own history.

No, there was nothing like that taught, not even our own culture. There were no dances, there was no weaving, or no artefacts, no handicraft, there was nothing like that taught. Nothing at all. That is what made me think that maybe if I was a captain in the ship, I would direct it in a different direction. And when I came to Townsville, this idea came into being, after I met all these different people.

*

**Noel Loos**: In Townsville in the late 1970s a group of Torres Strait Islanders, among them Koiki Mabo and Seriana Tapim, suggested that one organisation be formed to represent all of Townsville's Islander population. As a result Magani Malu Kes was formed. *Magani* in the Western, Central and Eastern Islands means Torres Strait. *Malu* is Western Island for 'deep water', and *Kes* is Eastern Island for 'passage' or 'strait'. Thus the name symbolically incorporated the three island groupings. Magani Malu Kes continued to be an important organisation for the large Torres Strait Islander community in Townsville for many years.

In August 1978 Mabo presented on behalf of the Black Community School a successful funding proposal to the Australian Institute of Aboriginal Studies to enable him to explore the possibility of the establishment of the Magani Institute. This was a wide-ranging proposal concerned primarily with matters of educational and cultural significance. Mabo suggested it become the parent organisation for the Black Community School and other such Torres Strait Islander schools, which Mabo envisaged developing in the near future at Mackay and even on Murray Island, although each school would be run by a Parents Council. Typically, Mabo proposed 'that the Magani Institute shall consider the possible erection of a school at Dam, near Las, on the site of the place of the traditional education of the youth of Mer'. The proposal was a rejection of the education provided for Islanders by the Queensland Government. The inclusion of Mer made this especially clear as there was already a state school there for the Meriam people, Mabo being one of its graduates.

Mabo highlighted a number of areas of concern for the Magani Institute. Not surprisingly, the mastery of English was a top priority. On behalf of the Black Community School, he wrote:

> We propose that the need for special attention to the needs of Torres Strait Islander children learning English in school in Australia be extensively studied by the Magani Insitute, and that the Magani Institute provide expertise for other community groups seeking solutions to the general problems of English literacy among Torres Strait Islander children.

One section entitled 'Curriculum' indicated how:

> The Magani Institute shall develop curricular materials for use in teaching traditional languages and culture, both within constituent schools and in other schools where learning about Torres Strait Islanders is desired.

The mastery of English was to be assisted by the development of resources to teach English as a second language to Torres Strait children and adults, using Torres Strait Islander Kriol, *Brokan*, as the language of instruction:

[Brokan is] the *lingua franca* of the Strait and … the primary language of most of the Torres Strait Islander children. It is also the principal language of several Torres Strait Islander communities, and of many of the Torres Strait Islanders now living in Australia.

There were a number of services listed for the Magani Institute to provide: educational consultation, an information centre about all things Torres Strait Islander, a translation service, an information service for Islanders about white Australian culture (*kolé ra tonar*), a community service linking government agencies and Torres Strait Islander people, a Magani Institute housing fund, administered by the community services section to ensure all Islanders were provided with adequate housing, and a Magani Institute research centre to conduct or contract research needed by government agencies and other bodies.

A substantial part of the proposal dealt with 'cultural studies' under the headings: academic research, sacred sites, traditional ownership, genealogy, and cultural materials. Mabo's proposal aimed at researching, describing, restoring and maintaining traditional and contemporary Torres Strait Islander culture as well as promoting commercial opportunities for Torres Strait Islander creativity.

The proposal for the establishment of the Magani Institute is imaginative and challenging even in 1996, and worthy of further consideration. Seen in the context of 1978 it is quite extraordinary. The Bjelke-Petersen Government was in power. It had just defied the Fraser Coalition Government in Canberra over outstations and increased autonomy for Aboriginal people on Mornington Island and Aurukun, and there seemed no prospect for land rights in Queensland. Yet from the small group of people associated with the Black Community School, this proposal was drafted. Once again Mabo and his supporters were years ahead of their time and the seed fell upon stony ground.

Mabo's other successful application for funding to the Australian Institute of Aboriginal Studies was submitted in November 1984. It was focused on recording the traditional boundaries determining land ownership on Murray Island and the sacred sites, especially those associated with the Malo-Bomai cult.

The Magani Institute proposal was obviously worked over at great length, typed and presented with a cool, academic professionalism. The 1984 proposal is rushed and handwritten in order to get the funding so that Mabo could work through January and February 1985 while he was on his university vacation. During this time there was to be a tombstone unveiling that would bring many Islanders back to Mer whom Mabo could consult. He was also trying to accomplish as much as possible before the Services legislation accompanying the Queensland Deeds of Grant in Trust legislation came into operation. Moreover, the mapping of traditional boundaries would be important in the native title High Court challenge and would provide him with a wonderful opportunity to discuss all of these matters with the Murray Islanders. In the extracts below, Mabo's determination that young Torres Strait Islanders and future generations would know their inheritance is poignantly expressed.

The aim of this project is to carry out the recording of Traditional Boundaries of
1. Tribal Areas
2. Clan land
3. Individual or family land
4. Sacred sites

5. Restoration of Shrines and Zogos of each tribe & clan groups.

Traditionally in the Torres Strait land has been owned & occupied quite differently from the land ownership by the Aboriginal people on the mainland. Therefore it would be necessary to carry out this project in several sequences; for instance, stage one would be to hold a public meeting and inform the Public of Mer the reasons for such a project to be undertaken and ask for their cooperation.

No such recordings have ever been done at all. It is most important that this type of recording be done at this stage before the New Qld Govt's Services Legislation takes its full effect, and it would be disastrous if none of this type of information is passed on to our future generations.

This type of information would also be of help to young Islanders born on the mainland through no fault of their own. This generation having no first hand experiences of Mer (Is) would no doubt find themselves in a difficult position of identifying themselves with their particular land. Recording of such land can also become a useful resource material for use in schools and colleges. It has become necessary that we as Islanders carry out these projects ourselves, because we feel the Torres Strait area and its people are of no academic interest to professional researchers. Therefore large institutions on the mainland hold very little information about our people and their culture.

This Project will enable me to document boundaries and sacred sites of Malo-Bomai Cult of Mer. It will be very beneficial to the people of Mer. As stated earlier such boundaries will be forgotten in the next twenty years or so because of the New Qld Act and the transmigration of Islanders to the North Qld cities on the mainland Qld. This could be the start of a major project which could spread across the whole of the Strait. We have some Islanders in Townsville who have been here for thirty years & their descendants have no knowledge of their traditional lands. It is important for these young-sters to understand their traditional heritage before it is lost forever.

My reference to this 'exciting and important proposal' is also handwritten and rushed. The extract below catches some of the urgency:

> I have known Mr Mabo very well since 1967 when we were both involved in the Inter-Racial Seminar held in Townsville: 'We the Australians: What Is to Follow the Referendum?' During this time Mr Mabo has shown an unshakable commitment to fostering the survival and growth of his Torres Strait Islander culture in the changed circumstances of the present and future. His development and implementation of the concept of the Black Community School in Townsville over so many years is proof of this, in part, if proof is needed. Mr Mabo has been a student of mine this semester. During this time he has recorded the history of the Mabo clan and has been appointed my part-time research assistant to flesh out that history.

*

**Noel Loos**: The Mabo Papers reveal a more complex, spiritual dimension to the political activist in these last years. In a short speech of welcome delivered to the first National Torres Strait

Islander Conference in Brisbane, 22–25 June 1991, Mabo clearly referred to God in typically Christian terms that his large Islander audience could relate to:

> Welcome to all my friends and delegates and a very good morning to all of you. Welcome to all leaders and spokespeople and employees. Most of us have travelled long distances. I welcome and appreciate your determination to be here at this conference. Despite the fact that you may have had very important tasks to do back home with your organisations … I also thank Our Heavenly Father for assisting Iina in their endeavours to get us together at this most critical time. And most of all many thanks to Iina Board of Directors and the staff who made it possible for us to come together today as one people.
>
> I would also like to express my sympathy to those … who had left us and departed to new life beyond. I wish that sweet memories of their association with us will remain with us for ever. For those of us remaining must strive to achieve the utmost for our people, while sharing love and continued friendship with our people.

The speech, made seven months before his death, has the ring of confidence of one who is an accepted leader of his people and feels at one with them. He had refused to attend unless his wife's fare to the conference was met. It was.

On 15 March 1988 at what Koiki vainly hoped would be the final hearing of *Mabo and Others, Mer Island's Traditional Land Claims* before the Full Bench of the High Court in Canberra, he made a moving entry. It expressed the tension and spiritual dimension of the occasion:

The writ for this case was issued in 1981 by the plaintiff. All of the hearing has been won by us. I hope my *Agud* will still be with me on these final days of our Land Claims: I know *Agud* will be with me.

In the privacy of his diary his expression of faith reached back past the Christianity of colonialism to the source of spiritual power revealed to his ancestors.

To the outside world Koiki Mabo was the quintessential political activist. He spoke to small and large groups, black and white, about Aboriginal and Islander advancement and of the essential place of the Meriam Traditional Land Claim to this movement. He also prepared a series of notices or handouts to increase the support begun at the 1981 Conference held at James Cook University when the Islanders decided to take their High Court action. Mabo utilised press commentary on the legal process to present the Islander case and his own unique political perspective. He used an article in *The Sydney Morning Herald* on 30 April 1985, 'Islanders Take White Australia to the High Court', to create a very effective one-page notice introducing himself to a wider audience and attacking the Queensland Government for its opposition to the Meriam claim to native title. He explained and rejected the *Coast Islands Declaratory Act*, which the Queensland Government passed in 1985 especially to defeat the Meriam High Court challenge. Mabo pointed to the racist motivation of this law. The journalist referred to it as 'apparently unprecedent'. Mabo also attacked the Queensland Government's Deeds of Grant in Trust Legislation, passed in 1984 to acknowledge for the first time in Queensland's history that Aboriginal and Torres Strait Islander people had some sort of title to their land. This was the National Party's attempt to placate the Aboriginal Advancement League, which had threatened to destroy Queensland's international reputation at the 1982 Brisbane Commonwealth Games. The Deeds of Grant in Trust were given to Queensland's Aboriginal and Torres Strait Islander communities by 1987. Only Murray Island refused to accept the Trust Deeds because of the pending High Court challenge and the uncertainty about how the Queensland offer would affect the Islanders' claim.

The *Herald* article quoted Mabo:

> The Government has long used Islanders to boost the economy of this State. This included cheap labour they took from my father.
>
> Now they are trying to stop us having land we are entitled to … My family has occupied the land for hundreds of years before Captain Cook was born. They are now trying to say I cannot own it.

Some elements of the national media had sensed the ramifications of the struggle that had been joined. A splendid photograph of Mabo accompanied the article while a map showed readers where Murray Island is situated. Above and below the article was Mabo's address to Torres Strait Islander people:

> Hi,
>
> My name is Edward Mabo, my island name is <u>Koiki</u>. I was born at Mer (Murray Island). I now live in Townsville. I will be returning soon to my home island to live.
>
> In this paper cutting, you will read about the test case I am heading on our behalf in the High Court of Australia.

If this case comes in our favour, this would mean we will not be paying rent to the DNA [Department of Native Affairs] anymore. As our islands will become recognised by Queensland Government as our own private land.

On the 9th April 1985 Queensland Government made a new law which will enable Aboriginal and Island people to lease traditional lands. They also passed another law which says that after we became part of Queensland in 1879, we lost our rights to our land and no compensation will be claimed by us. We admit that we became part of Queensland in 1879 but our land rights exist and we want our rights to be fully recognised by the Queensland Government. Because we believe these laws are made by men and can be undone by men.

Present Queensland Government is a friendly enemy of the black people as they like to give you the Bible and take away your land.

We should stop calling them Boss and we should not give them our respect.

This is an edited and abridged extract of
*Edward Koiki Mabo: His Life and Struggle for Land Rights*
by Noel Loos and Eddie Koiki Mabo,
published by University of Queensland Press, 1996.

# Q&A

## Jimi Bani

**Q**: Tell me a little about yourself.

**A**: I was born and raised on Waibene, Thursday Island, in the Torres Strait. My tribal groups are Wagadagam, Mabuyag Island, in the near western part of Torres, and Peiudu, Erub Island, in the eastern part of Torres Strait. My totems are crocodile and frigate bird. My constellation is the shark and my wind is the north-west wind. I also always like to acknowledge my bloodline connections to Solomon Islands, Rotuma, and Butchulla and Kaurareg nations.

I'm the eldest of six boys. I have a big family and grew up practising culture, Island custom and Christianity – church every Sunday. If you ask how important family is to me, I'd say family is who I am. Growing up, my role models were my grandparents on both sides, my parents and my uncles and aunties. I was fortunate enough to be raised by a village. I have five children now and even with all my work on film and stage, this is one of the highlights of my life so far.

**Q**: What was school like for you?

**A**: I went to Tamwoy kindergarten, Thursday Island State Primary School and Thursday Island State High School, now known as Tagai State College. It was great. Always surrounded by family and cousins. We didn't have very much growing up, so sharing was a big thing for us, from food to clothes. In primary school, traditional Island dancing and Wednesday afternoon basketball competition were the things I looked forward to the most, and it carried through to high school. Everything was all about sports: athletics, rugby league, basketball and volleyball.

So there are many stories. But if there's a memory I can share now, it's how when I was in primary school, a couple of times I got chosen to manually ring the school bell! Yes, that's right: ringing the school bell manually hahaha ... this was obviously just before the electric school bell arrived. Just knowing when the break time was coming closer, and the teacher would say 'Jimi' and give me the nod, and I'd get up, pack up my stuff, walk to the bell, and as I walked past the classes, the students knew what I was about to do, so they'd all start packing up their stuff – I tell you, it was a big thing, especially when lunch was over, students would crowd the bell ringer. Magic times!

**Q**: How did you get into acting?

**A**: First of all, I give credit to producer Penny Chapman, who encouraged me during the filming of the TV series *RAN: Remote Area Nurse* to go study the craft of acting. It was the best thing for my career. I ended up auditioning for drama schools around the country and I was fortunate enough to get a phone call from the head of acting at the Western Australian Academy of Performing Arts (WAAPA) at the time, Chris Edmund. He explained the structure of the course to me, and I got hooked. Not sure if they still have it, but there was this club which the second-year acting students ran called Club Fred, which fundraised for the third-year students so they could travel east to do their end-of-year showcase. They would also organise and look after the first-year students and make sure they were settled in. That structure got me.

**Q**: What was it like at WAAPA?

**A**: Look, at the start, I struggled. Not with the course, but because that was the longest I'd ever been away from home, and it was a huge culture shock for me. I was the only Indigenous fella in my class and for the first time I felt isolated. It took me a while to adjust, but not without the support, mentorship and friendship of writer/actor/producer Ian Meadows and his family. (He was in third-year acting at that time.)

I felt that Perth was home and settled in. Once I adjusted, it was not until our first general public show in second year that I was like, 'Okay this isn't so bad at all.' And also most importantly, my partner Idelia and son Dmitri moved over to Perth with me, and it was the best thing ever. We settled in, and then my focus became more on the craft. Through the years I also started building friendships and fell in love with storytelling and how to be a storyteller. Graduating was the best thing I've ever done. Not to mention that what I learnt at WAAPA was just top-level stuff. A valuable lesson I learned was 'Keep working on the craft of storytelling'.

A lot of the lecturers were great as well, and I saw them as mentors. Something one of them said stuck with me: 'When you graduate, trust me, it will be the best thing you'll ever do. You've got so much to offer in this industry, you just need the tools.'

**Q**: You've appeared in a range of TV, movie and stage productions. What work are you most proud of?

**A**: I've been fortunate enough to work on many amazing and important projects. Each project had a purpose, whether it was a story that needed to be told, or a challenge for me that developed me as an actor.

*Jandamarra* was the first show I ever did out of WAAPA, playing a resistance fighter from Bunuba Country in the Kimberley. I was so honoured to play the role and learn the history. An important approach we took in *Jandamarra* became a structure I have practised in every role I play. It was the cultural consultation process. Meeting the community and families. Getting the blessing of the elders and ancestors. To understand if it is a 'yes' or a 'no' from them, and to respect that decision.

The film *Mabo* was special. An important story to be told. Such a privilege and honour to work with the family. Also working with Deborah Mailman and Rachel Perkins lifted my craft to another level.

Our show *My Name Is Jimi* was very special as well, a show about my family connections, our cultural kod structure and the language of the Wagadagam tribe, Mabuyag Island. I also had my mum, my grandma, my two brothers and my son on stage with me telling the story.

**Q**: What advice would you give to a young Jimi Bani, starting out on a career in the performing arts?

**A**: Invest in yourself before investing in others.

**Q**: How do you maintain your strong Torres Strait Islander culture and identity?

**A**: Practise it daily and implement it in storytelling format. It's really challenging when you are surrounded by a culture and system that is not yours. I'd like to share a quote from my late grandfather, Ephraim Bani: 'Culture will change and adapt, however, we must be very careful that we don't lose our identity.'

# The Smell of Sugar Cane

## Aaron Fa'Aoso with Michelle Scott Tucker

Dad's funeral was held in the familiar, austere church that my family attended each week in Cairns. Grandad's funeral was held there too, only two weeks later.

I don't remember too much about the service, but I do remember leaning into the casket to give him a kiss. It shocked me how cold Dad's lips were, and I knew right then that whoever was in that casket was not my father.

If I felt grief, I was too young to recognise it. I just felt lonely. The bright, sunny little boy that I was before Dad died became a sadder and quieter child.

As the eldest son, I was the man of the house now. Mum and Nan probably never said it out loud, but lots of other family members did. I was only six, and it was a lot for a kid that young, but I took it on and took it seriously. Besides, on the night of the second funeral, Grandad's funeral, I had a vivid dream. Dad and Grandad came to me and Grandad said, 'You gotta take care of your grandmother and your mother. It's all on you now.'

39

From then on, I feel like I never really had a childhood. I carried the weight of my responsibilities, even as – consciously or otherwise – I was frustrated by my inability to protect and care for Mum and Nan in any meaningful way. It's like I was born with protector DNA, born a guard dog trying to keep the wolves out.

With three little boys, Mum struggled to manage – and who wouldn't – although her grandmother, my Dhudhu, was a solid support to her, as was the gospel. Nan, my mother's mother, helped when she could, but she was engulfed by her own grief too. There was a deep sadness in the family for a long time, a sadness that we never spoke about. On an emotional level, things were never quite right, ever again.

My mum wasn't one of those parents who let you get away with anything. She was so tough that I lived in fear of her a lot of the time, but she rarely raised her voice; when I was in trouble, it was still all calm.

'Hey, son,' she'd say, and that's all she needed to say for me to know that *Ohhhhh, she's mad. I'm gunna get my arse kicked.* Or slapped or smacked or, sometimes, belted with an actual belt.

Once, when I was still pretty young, I took some chocolate from the corner shop. My younger brother James saw and, when I refused to share it with him, he dobbed me in to Mum. She didn't get mad. She accepted that children do those sorts of things. But she made me walk back in and tell the shop owner I'd stolen it. 'You take it back,' she said in her quiet way, 'and you tell the man what you did.'

Oh my God, the shame.

That stuff really stuck, and I reckon that's why I never went on to have a career in breaking and entering. Later, in my teens, when some friends' hijinks escalated into outright theft,

I stepped away because I knew how Mum was going to be if she found out. All my rebellious teenage crap would be about fighting. I never so much as took a bike for a joy ride, because I knew perfectly well that Mum would have made me take it back and apologise.

Even thinking about that scenario makes me sweat. I can picture Mum knocking at a bewildered stranger's door.

'My son, he stole this from you ... What do you wanna say, Aaron?'

'I'm sorry.'

'Yeah, you're a big man now, aren't you Aaron?'

'Sorry.'

'Back in the car, Aaron!'

That's Mum's superpower right there: making me feel remorse for an imaginary crime! I was deadset scared of her, and of Nan too. Also, and probably more to the point, I didn't want to be a disappointment. That was the biggest thing, far beyond avoiding physical punishment.

I grew up in a household with high expectations. High, high. I mean HIGH. Mum had us listening to recordings of Dr Martin Luther King, and the bar doesn't get any higher than that. Mum and Nan were also massive on how we had to present ourselves in public. Our shirts, our pants, everything immaculate: we had to look good, and we had to behave good, too. We weren't only representing ourselves; we were representing the household. If you're going to be a man, this is what we expect of a man. They scared me into being a man. Stand up, damn it, this is where the bar is. And I knew. I knew where the bar was set. It wasn't the physical that had me worried, it was the fear of letting Mum and Nan down. Which, of course, I inevitably went on to do.

The very first time I let Mum down, though, probably wasn't my fault – which didn't make it one bit easier to bear. When I was about ten, Mum took up with another man. Like my dad, this new bloke was Tongan, and at least part of what Mum found attractive in him was his ability to provide a Tongan outlook to us boys.

But he was bad news, often violent towards Mum, and I hated him. I never saw him hit her, but we could hear muffled sounds from the next room whenever he gave her a flogging. While the beatings were going on, Dhudhu would hold James and me in her arms, trying to comfort us. Each flogging felt like it lasted an eternity.

It was agony, and soon I stopped staying at or even going around to Mum's place: I stayed put at Nan's. Even there, though, I didn't escape the fallout. The former partner of Mum's new boyfriend lived not far from Nan's place, and she and her family knew who I was. It's fair to say they were pretty unhappy about this bloke moving in with my mother. Seriously, you'd think they'd have been pleased to see him gone. Anyway, there were some boys living in the former partner's house, all a few years older than me. I had to walk past their place on my way to and from school and they'd gather outside and talk shit and bully me as I went past. They never physically hurt me; it was just always awkward.

Before too long, the new bloke and Mum decided to move from Cairns to Canberra, where Mum could have a better job. But I refused to go with them. I flat out refused. I said it in front of him, too. I didn't like him, and I wasn't going to go. Presumably there were arguments – I don't remember now – but Mum's solution was to take my brothers and leave me behind. Nan and I were gutted.

In hindsight, as an adult, I get that Mum wasn't able to think clearly. Grieving for her husband and her dad, victimised by the new bloke, battling to make ends meet – she probably felt like she had no choice. Perhaps she didn't; he was quite the control freak. I hold no ill-feeling for whatever decision she made then or was forced to make. She wasn't in the right state of mind when she made those decisions, and I've since made similarly dubious decisions, going through my own grief. Unless you've walked a similar road, you can't understand.

What's more, for a black woman in the 1980s in Far North Queensland, the hurdles were even higher. It might be acceptable now to be a single parent, but back then it was frowned on. Add together her being a single mother and a Torres Strait Islander woman, and Mum wasn't just behind the eight ball – she was completely off the pool table. She was simply trying to make something of herself, and help her children succeed.

But at the time, all that was lost on me. Mum's decision to move to Canberra with my brothers broke my heart, and the pain of it is with me even now. I felt abandoned and, simultaneously, I hated myself for having no power to protect her. I was meant to be the man of the family, and even though I was only ten years old, I felt I'd let her down.

Mum left mid-year and I didn't end up seeing her or either of my brothers for six months or so. It was a dark and lonely time.

Don't get me wrong, I was happy with Nan, but I missed my brothers and my mum. So did Nan. At bedtime, she would sing me to sleep – songs from Zenadth Kes, the Torres Strait, most of them really sad, but I loved it. I guess when you live on an island and make a living from the sea, people are always leaving, maybe never to return, so the sad songs shouldn't be a surprise.

As a baby I was given to my Nan to be raised, in an informal Torres Strait adoption. And as my second mum, Nan has always been my harshest critic and my fiercest protector.

Once, when I was a little tacker in kindy class, my teacher decided to punish me for whatever silly thing it was I'd done. She removed me from the class and made me stay in the toilet, with the clear implication that I was a dirty little black kid and that was where I belonged. When Nan came to pick me up that day and heard what had happened, she turned the tables and it was the teacher who found herself on the receiving end of a lesson. Nan's never been one for holding anything back, and that teacher was left in no doubt as to what Nan thought of her and her disciplinary methods.

Anyway, when Christmas approached in that difficult year, Mum started to have second thoughts about her situation. The tipping point arrived when the new bloke threw a weighty and sharply pointed candle holder at her head. He missed, thank goodness, but it took a chunk out of the wall behind her. This wasn't the life she wanted, for herself or for her sons.

Careful not to alert her boyfriend that she was planning to leave, Mum gradually packed some essentials over a period of days. Then, one morning, she took the guy to the shops, told him she'd wait with the kids in the car, and left him there while she drove to a women's shelter. Mum, James and John were there, at the shelter, for Christmas Day. It was all right, she says now, because the boys were given presents and made a fuss of by the staff.

Typical Mum – as long as her sons were okay, she'd make the best of anything. She's a superhero, honestly.

Soon after, Mum started slowly heading back up north. She stopped over along the way with various friends and relations, and to this day remains grateful to the people who helped her.

Eventually Mum, my brothers, Nan and I all moved into the house that Mum still lives in, in the Cairns suburb of Woree. A modest brick bungalow furnished for comfort, full of family mementos and – in accordance with Mum's and Nan's high Islander standards – always scrupulously clean. In pride of place was the cabinet where Mum kept all our sporting trophies (later, she would move our trophies to the back, to make room for her grandchildren's). To this day Mum's house feels like home to me. And to this day I still take my shoes off at the door.

While Mum and Nan moving in together was a sensible solution, the effect of putting those two women under the same roof was not unlike applying a match to a couple of bottle rockets: you definitely got fireworks and noise. It worked most of the time until, you know, it didn't.

Both stubbornly alpha females, they operated differently but were similar in character. If Nan got worked up about something having to be a certain way, Mum would give in and do as Nan wanted, but then Mum wouldn't speak. For days!

The tension would be unbearable when Mum was in a funk. Honestly, she took being passive aggressive to another level. For those days, the whole house would be on mute, including all of us boys, because we knew she could erupt at any moment, and until then we were all walking around on tiptoes. Mum could break down an SAS soldier with that silent treatment, I swear.

When Nan went crook, it was like a tropical storm: lightning, wind and noise before it's suddenly over and done with. But if Mum got angry, which luckily only happened rarely, it was the apocalypse. Then my brothers and I were like: *Mayday, mayday, mayday, let's get outta here!*

With some mates, we'd grab our pushies and go down the creek. It was a good distance away, maybe twenty kilometres, so by the time we'd ridden there we were dying for a swim. On the way, at the top of one particularly steep hill, there was a guava tree where we'd pause to catch our breath and grab a snack. Then we'd swoop down the hill to the creek and spend hours mucking around, talking rubbish and doing nothing much at all.

We tumbled down the rapids, swung on vines while making Tarzan noises, and dared each other to climb up to the highest ledges we could find before launching ourselves into the air and crashing into our favourite deep, still ponds. On the way back we'd pool our coins and buy a feed to share. Then home in time for dinner, or else Mum and Nan would be in my ear. Again.

What I love about Mum and Nan, though, was how they never blinked despite finding themselves widows. I take my hat off to Mum for what she did for us, because from the time she moved in with Nan we never wanted for anything. Always had fresh clothes on our backs, good food on our table. Sports uniforms, registration fees, bikes, schoolbooks, excursions – Mum and Nan somehow provided it all.

Looking back, I can see that our upbringing was sometimes difficult, sure, but I never felt like we were poor.

Now and again, as a special treat, Nan would take one of us boys down to the Esplanade in town to go fishing. It would take us a good hour to walk there, but Nan made it fun. I didn't have the patience for fishing with a handline, still don't, so while Nan would sit and wait for a nibble, I'd run off and play along the foreshore.

Sometimes on the way home we'd detour and, as part of the adventure, we'd collect mussels from among the mangroves that lined Chinaman Creek. It wasn't until I was an adult that I realised how necessary these adventures were to keeping us fed.

Some of my forefathers were canecutters, renowned for their skills and hard work, but as a boy I learnt that the toughest, strongest people in my life were my mum and nan.

Women of the Samu (cassowary) and Koedal (crocodile) clans, from the Torres Strait, Mum and Nan are proud descendants of generations of Melanesian warriors. Strong, and fierce with it, they are also the most loving women I know.

My nan, Mary-Betty Harris, was born on Saibai, a large, low-lying Australian island only four kilometres south of the Papua New Guinea mainland. In 1947, when Nan was a teenager, king tides flooded the island, submerging the main village under metres of water. For the people of Saibai, it was only the latest in a series of environmental challenges. The community had been suffering from the effects of erosion and the impact of salt on their crops and freshwater supplies for a long time.

After much discussion, many Saibai families decided to move permanently to the Australian mainland – to the tip of Cape York Peninsula, about 170 kilometres south. By the early 1950s, a settlement was established, called Bamaga in honour of the Elder, Bamaga Ginau, who had led the migration discussions but not lived to see the results.

Basically, my nan and her family were Australia's first climate-change refugees.

For almost twenty years, Nan lived in Bamaga with her family, and then with Grandad. She had a daughter – her only child, Delilah Elizabeth, my mum. Nan was determined that her girl would receive a solid education. So in 1968, when Mum was thirteen, Nan and Grandad moved south again, this time to Cairns, so Mum could go to school there.

In the 1960s and early '70s, Cairns was a country town of about 30,000 people. It was a thousand kilometres away from Bamaga and a world away in terms of educational and work opportunities. Mum and Nan's story – and mine too, I guess – is in many ways a typical migrant tale of having to move from a cherished homeland to a place that offered – well, to a place that offered more.

The loneliness, the difficulties of being black newcomers in a largely white community, that sense of not quite fitting in – it was all a loving sacrifice, leaving family and friends for the benefit of the children, and of their children to come.

And although our family life became sombre when Dad and Grandad passed away, it wasn't all bleak. There was a lot of love, with plenty of good moments.

My brothers, our mates and I roamed Cairns' streets and parks and surrounding countryside as a pack. We came to know each nook and cranny, each hidey-hole under a bridge.

Except on Henleys Hill, a scrub-covered rise a few streets away from my house. Everyone knew that a hairyman lurked there – a yowie, a bigfoot – and we avoided going near if we could help it. Aside from that though, we knew our area inside and out, knew it was all ours and never took for granted how beautiful it was.

If we didn't ride our bikes to the creek, we rode up and down the street, playing a game we called 'gauntlet'. We'd grab brooms, mops or long-handled garden tools and the idea was to throw them, spear-like, at the wheels of a passing bike. If the broom got caught in the spokes and caused the rider to crash onto the asphalt road surface, then that was a win. There was no malice to it, we all thought it was funny, and the biggest stacks received the loudest cheers. I remember happily picking myself up off the road, casually inspecting my new grazes, and then enthusiastically finding a mop I could chuck at one of my mates.

For years Mum worked an afternoon shift which ended at midnight so she could be there for us each morning. Through her work ethic, and by standing proud, Mum showed us boys that we came from a family with a passion for work, and for working hard. She went above and beyond to ensure we didn't miss out.

Mum made sure we always took a couple of special trips each year, during the school holidays. South to Townsville for the Christmas holidays, when we'd always stay with Nan's brother. During the June–July holidays we'd head north to Bamaga to stay with and see more family and friends.

Families in Zenadth Kes culture are anything but insular – not confined to Mum plus Dad plus kids. It's normal, and good, for kids to be close to members of their extended family. I had cousins, uncles and aunties in Bamaga who were around my age and who were like siblings to me, genuinely just like brothers and sisters. We bickered, we teased each other, we supported and advised each other and, most of all, we loved each other. No matter what. In turn, those who were Mum's age, or Nan's, treated me like a son – feeding me, sheltering me, advising me and, all too often, growling at me as well!

One of Nan's maternal uncles and his family lived on five acres in Aloomba, about thirty minutes south of Cairns. For everyone who had moved south from the Torres Strait to Cairns and the surrounding towns, Nadi Anu and Yaba Anu's property was the Samu clan's HQ – a place of gladness and belonging.

All my cousins, uncles and aunties spent time at Aloomba: visiting and yarning, playing and running around. On special occasions – birthday parties, tombstone ceremonies, christenings, engagements, weddings, shaving ceremonies – sometimes more than a hundred adults would gather, with at least another hundred children. All of us together felt like thousands to me.

Aloomba was surrounded by cane fields and the pungent smell of the cane remains, for me, the scent of childhood and connection.

The kids would play nonstop and, within those five acres, dense with tropical trees, undergrowth and vines, a game like hide-and-seek could go on for joyful hours. Sometimes we'd go out roaming in a gang, walking beside and between the cane fields, pausing to break off a sweet, juicy stem to suck on, and playing a game called 'finding snakes'. Seriously, that was the entire game. (I know, right?) Luckily, we were pretty bad at it, and never found one.

The nearby Behana Creek, shallow with a sandy bed, was our swimming place, and the Mulgrave River was where my uncles used to take the older boys to learn how to spear dive. That was a true rite of passage and I loved to tag along and watch. Us little ones weren't allowed to dive, but we could hold the rope strung with fish and keep an eye out for crocs. You had to listen carefully and not mess up, otherwise you weren't allowed to go next time. As the uncles caught more fish, the rope got heavier and heavier, but we wouldn't dream of complaining. The uncles made us littlies feel like men too, although we were worse than useless.

I was so useless that one afternoon when we returned from the river, I loaded the speargun and, thinking it was a good joke, pointed it at my mum. Oooh boy – not a good joke. Mum gave me a hiding that I've never forgotten, and I cried like a baby. What's worse, she did it in front of everyone, so the embarrassment hurt even more.

When I was a bit older, us kids would head across town after school to the training studio where we were learning martial arts. During the first half of the year, we'd ride there on our pushies but later in the year – during sugarcane harvest – we could sometimes hitch a ride on a cane train.

The train line ran around what was then the outskirts of Cairns, with the locos hauling bins of freshly cut sugar cane to the mill. The really long trains – those pulling eighty bins or more – moved slowly enough to make it possible to jump on and off the last few bins, and fast enough to make it a bit of a dangerous challenge. To our minds, it was much more fun than the bus we might otherwise take and it was more convenient too, because the cane trains ran 24/7 during the crushing season.

The train people didn't like us doing it, though, and sometimes they'd set a guard to ride the bins and keep kids like us away. For those guards, we invented a new game, called 'chase'. If we'd decided the game was on, we'd be deliberately cheeky to provoke a reaction. Then we'd run. That's when our knowledge of the landscape, of every nook and cranny and every hidey-hole, came in handy. We'd miss the train – couldn't catch it if a guard was riding it anyway – but the laughs we had while evading the train guards made up for it.

Still laugh, just thinking about it.

It was an enormous comfort to me, growing up, that the Torres Strait community in the Cairns area was so strong. Since childhood, my life has been a constant round of family and community gatherings – Christian rituals where we come together to affirm our bonds, followed by delicious feasts and celebrations that confirmed my Zenadth Kes identity, culture and language.

My Zenadth Kes world, though, was quite separate from the white Australian world of school or what I watched on TV.

Popular culture didn't reflect my life or my family, so I took my cues wherever I could find them. During the 1980s, the West Indian cricket team was unbeatable. They were outstanding sportsmen, beloved by all Australians, and they were cool. So cool, man. For a while there, I regularly spoke with what I hoped was a Caribbean accent. Best of all, they all looked like they could be my uncles. It was one of the first times I could watch a whole team of black men, on TV, all being celebrated for what they could achieve.

It speaks to the importance of representation, doesn't it? At last, I was seeing 'myself' in popular culture, and that was incredibly significant. Crucial to me as a boy and directly relevant to the work I do now to increase the stories and representation of First Nations people in the film and television industry. It's true, I reckon: you can't be what you don't see. Media is a powerful industry, and it can be used to change hearts and minds. That's what motivates me now.

These days I don't have time for pushbikes, or for martial arts. Board meetings, production meetings, workshops, film sets, dinner functions, budgets, reports, scripts, phone calls and of course emails – so many bloody emails!

Sometimes though, when I arrive home to Cairns after yet another interstate trip, I can smell sugar cane in the air as I step outside the airport terminal.

And every time – every single time, despite everything – it makes me pause and it makes me smile.

# *One Culture*

### Rhett Loban

My name is Rhett Loban and I was born in Brisbane on Turrbal Country. I was raised in both a Torres Strait and Scottish household. My father, Gehamat Loban, was born on Waiben or Thursday Island, however, we also have connections to Mabuyag and Boigu. Growing up as a Torres Strait Islander born on the mainland, I have learnt about many aspects of Torres Strait culture throughout my life. From everyday inter- actions such as walking out of the house to meet and greet visitors and farewelling them as they leave, to more significant events such as tombstone openings, to stories about the Dogai (female spirit). However, aspects of my cultural heritage that were always presented as an integral part of Torres Strait iden- tity were Indonesian and broader Malay cultural practices.

I know from my father that our family has links back to Banda Neira, Timor and Singapore. These memories and knowledge come from his family, relations and reminiscences of growing up, as well as looking back through the family tree. In our household, I was always taught about both local Islander culture, and Indonesian and Malay culture. Stories about the Dogai were told along with those about Pontianak; words like makan ('to eat' or 'food') were used interchangeably with kai kai (also 'to eat'), and semur was cooked alongside sop sop. For my family, these were all part of a distinctly Torres Strait culture.

Speaking with friends and others from Singapore, Malaysia and Indonesia, I have found that there are words and customs that we share, and these cultural commonalities often surprised them. There are differences too, but these shared customs confirm that aspects of Torres Strait culture reflect influences from the Malay Archipelago, creating a culture that is distinct to the Torres Strait. For example, the word dato as used in the Torres Strait is not always spelt the same as in Indonesian or Malay languages, nor is it necessarily a direction translation. My family and I have always used dato as a word for grandfather, and I have always known that this was one of the words in the Torres Strait used for grandfather (another is athe). However, from my interactions with Indonesian, Malaysian and Singaporean peoples, I have learnt that the word is also used for a respected person or a leader. This use of the word is in part similar to the Torres Strait, as we use the words dato and puman within the community as titles of respect. Datos and pumans are both well respected within the community, but datos are more senior than pumans. We also use other Indonesian words for family in a community context, such as the word for bebe (aunty), nene (grandmother), pache (uncle), kaka (eldest sister), and abung (eldest brother). To this day, the word dato is used to refer to both grandfather and/or a respected person in the community.

A story told to me by my father is one about Pontianak, a spirit woman who targets young men at night. In the story

I was told, she lived in the frangipani tree; however, in discussions with others from the Malay Archipelago, I have heard she lives in a banana tree or a banyan tree. In stories from outside the Torres Strait, the scent of frangipani follows her wherever she goes. In Indonesian and Malay stories, she is a young woman who died before her time or during childbirth, and has become a vampiric spirit. Some of the details are different, but the general story is the same and the link can be seen between the Torres Strait narrative and narratives from the rest of the Malay Archipelago.

Some of these aspects of Indonesian and wider Malay culture have become universal within Torres Strait culture, with even those from non-Indonesian/Malay families absorbing and sharing knowledge and cultural practices between communities. For example, semur is a well-known and common dish from the Torres Strait that is recognised by many Islanders. This dish possibly originates from the Malay Archipelago, and it varies within Indonesia and the Torres Straits. My great dato was from Banda Neira, a spice island, and in our semur dish we add nutmeg and cloves, which are ingredients not necessarily added by other Torres Strait families, or possibly even by Indonesian and broader Malay communities. However, the semur dish has a chicken, vermicelli and soy sauce base and is widespread among the Torres Strait community.

Our family also prepares dishes from other cultures within the Torres Strait, such as dinuguan, which is pork cooked in pigs' blood. This dish seems to have originated in the Philippines, and Filipino families in the Torres Strait likely introduced the dish. Similarly, namas may have originated from the Japanese dish namasu (pickled food), likely introduced by Japanese pearl-shell divers. To make namas in the Torres Straits, the fish is pickled and cooked by soaking thin pieces in vinegar and lime juice. Even though my family connections and heritage are not directly linked to either the Philippines or Japan, these dishes are widely known and prepared in the Torres Strait. Some Indonesian and Malay words are used to describe different dishes and foods including chopi (steamed chicken and vegetable dish), sambal (which can be a condiment or a substantial dish using squid, pearl meat, mango or another base), blachan (shrimp paste), ekan (fish), babi (pork), ayam (chicken) and nasi (rice). Just as sop sop is a traditional dish local to the islands, these dishes have also become a part of Torres Strait culture.

Often culture and food go hand in hand. After the passing of a loved one or community member, my great dato and the other Muslim men gathered for feasts at seven, forty and one hundred days after the person's passing. I am told these gatherings were initially for Muslim men and their grandsons. Food was set on white sheets, sometimes with another layer of palm-leaf mats underneath. The food, sheets and mats were spread on the floor and attendees sat cross-legged. At the beginning of the ceremony, the adults prayed and burnt incense, and fruit, cakes and tea were served first and the feast held later. The men often placed or tied a cloth over their heads. Later in the ceremony, the men distributed coins to the grandsons as presents. Following this, the rest of the community were invited to partake in the feast. I have been told that at other feasting events, males and females had particular roles in planning and cooking for the celebration. The girls and women also learnt culture though dances such as the handkerchief dance, the clapstick dance with bamboo poles, and the fan dance.

I have been told that the tombstone-opening ceremony evolved out of Muslim and Malay burial practices. In Muslim and Malay burial customs in the Torres Strait, the deceased is wrapped in white cloth, and leftover sheets are torn into strips, which are then wrapped around the wrists of family members and friends. Mourners keep this strip of cloth on their wrists for one hundred days or until it falls off. Moreover, during the forty days of mourning after the death, there is no music or radio. These practices coincided with the previously mentioned feasts at seven, forty and one hundred days after the death. The end of the mourning period aligns with the tombstone-opening ceremony, which is often held long after the person has passed away, a year or two years, or whenever the family can afford to hold the event. In many tombstone openings, Muslim burial practices are blended with Islander customs, including the use of artefacts such as the wap (Torres Strait harpoon), warup (Torres Strait drum) and mats or other objects that are placed at the grave prior to the ceremony. The headstone is wrapped, and money is sometimes pinned within the wrapping. Cleaning and maintaining the grave are the duties of the family, a custom which I understand was also practised in other places in the Malay Archipelago in the past. In these cases, the mourning timeframe and Malay burial practices aligned with those of the tombstone opening. The Malay burial practices have been influenced by Island culture, with Islander artefacts used in the ceremony in some cases. For some Islanders, the tombstone opening and Muslim and Malay burial practices are one and the same.

Many aspects of Indonesian and broader Malay culture continue in Torres Strait culture in some form today. From significant events such as tombstone openings to everyday foods such as sambal and the use of Malay language in Torres Strait Creole. Many people in my family and the broader Torres Strait community continue to use naming conventions such as dato, bebe, abung, kaka and other titles of respect. I hope to continue these traditions and cultural practices, passing this knowledge and way of life down to the next generation.

In writing this short piece, I am sharing my own experiences and learnings growing up Torres Strait Islander. The vibrant, rich and multicultural history of the Torres Strait has informed Torres Strait culture today. While it may seem that the Indonesian and broader Malay community influenced the local Island community, this process has in fact been a two-way exchange, with the Indonesian and wider Malay community marrying and becoming part of the local Islander community and taking on the Islander way of life.

These cultural influences of the Indonesian and the wider Malay community have helped to shape the Torres Strait culture and identity that we have today. For many, these Indonesian and Malay cultural practices, traditions and more are inseparable from Torres Strait culture: they are one culture.

## My Father, Francis 'The Hatman' Wapau – Master Weaver

### Lockeah Wapau

My name is Lockeah Wapau. My parents are Francis (deceased) and Denise Wapau (née Sabbo). I was born in Brisbane and raised in Mackay, Queensland, in a beach suburb called Bucasia. I have an older sibling, Juleian.

These are some of my dearest recollections of my upbringing by my father and growing up as a Torres Strait Islander in mainland Australia.

My father, Francis 'Frank' Wapau, was also known in North Queensland market circles as 'The Hatman', and as 'Friday' on the Cairns Esplanade.

My Torres Strait Islander heritage lies with my father's parents. My late grandfather was Ned 'Daruga' Wapau of the Ait Cadul people of Saibai Island, and my late grandmother was Kelem 'Mumma' Wapau (née Akee) of the Zagareb/Geuram clans of Murray Island. Dad had three siblings, his older sister, Cecelia (deceased), and his brothers, Kokwam and Abia (deceased).

My mother's heritage lies with the Sugar Slaves or 'Kanakas' of North Queensland, tying my roots to ancestors from Malaita in the Solomon Islands and Epi in Vanuatu, and and the Aboriginal Kalkadoon people of central western Queensland.

Although I have not travelled back to the Torres Strait, I am proud to say that I am a Torres Strait Islander. I was lucky and fortunate that I was raised in my culture and heavily influenced by my late father. Raised on Bucasia Beach, I was taught by my father about our amazing Torres Strait Islander culture, especially our connection to the sea, at an early age. Dad was one of a kind and a trailblazer in displaying our amazing culture in North Queensland and interstate.

My earliest recollection of Dad is that he was tall and lean but solid in build, probably from the good Island diet he consumed. He was the perfect dad. Funny and kind, he always looked at the brighter side of life. His smile and laugh would light up a room.

Dad's last paying occupation I recall was that he was employed as a high-voltage electrical linesman for the Queensland Electrical Commission from 1982 to 1991, and he was the first Indigenous linesman in the state. At this stage of his life, he felt he wanted to break the mould and be different. I can understand why Dad decided to finish as a linesman when he did, probably because he wanted to give working for himself a shot. In 1991 he decided to down tools. Using all his cultural knowledge, he began his business, Oriama Ait Artefacts.

If you did not know Dad, I'll let you know now. He was well known in North Queensland for his self-made cultural artefacts, especially his weaving. Not only in the Mackay market scene, but also in the surrounding towns of North Queensland. His hats were iconic.

My earliest recollection of the business was distributing fly-ers to neighbours' letterboxes, offering to collect coconuts and to trim the coconut fronds in their yards for free. It may seem funny now, but it's how Dad provided for our family. After getting numerous responses to the flyers, my older brother and I would accompany him in our white XC Ford Falcon. Dad would climb and cut the fronds and coconuts for me and my brother to collect. Afterwards, we would load up the car and cruise home with twenty fronds on the roof and coconuts in the boot with our dog. It was deadly! You would often see us driving along the streets of Bucasia, loaded up to the hilt. If it wasn't coconut fronds, we would be col-lecting bamboo from local cane farmers' paddocks to make spears, wall panels and Island drums, or collecting lawyer cane from the rainforest in the surrounding mountains to make cane baskets.

Oriama Ait Artefacts began under our house. This was Dad's studio and my classroom.

It was not like a whitefellas' art studio; it was different. It was like a factory. Dad had work schedules on the walls, showing what he needed to produce, when and where to get materi-als, and upcoming markets and events. There were numerous turtle shells hanging on the walls and traditional waps (bamboo spears) mounted on the ceiling. He made a homemade bar from bamboo. There was a table covered in handpainted coconuts and handwoven insects and animals. Out in the backyard, he had old bathtubs of coconut fronds soaking in water, a kup-murri (feast-ing ceremony) pit in the corner and an Island bamboo house he made, which served its purpose at Christmas time. Strands of lawyer cane were strewn across the backyard from the cane baskets he wove.

The front driveway was part of the studio too, as he would sit out there with his fronds and 'wok busket' and weave. He had it down pat, weaving three styles of hats, baskets, fruit bowls, children's toys, hand fans and animals for the weekend markets. It was at this time that he invented his iconic woven grasshopper, which is rarely produced now because of its intricate pattern.

It didn't stop at night-time; he would still be working under the house, painting the handwoven insects and animals for ceiling mobiles. He painted coconuts with Island landscapes and panoramic ocean views. On weeknights he worked late into the night until he was tired. With his cassette player playing, everything from the blues to rock-and-roll to '80s music would sound out from underneath the house most nights. His fingers kept the beat, weaving and painting.

Attending markets on the weekends was the best. He started out locally, with a stall at the Mackay Showground Markets. Never missing a Saturday, rain, hail or shine, he would be there wearing his floral Island shirt and signature 'Island sombrero'. In later years he moved from the showground and set up a permanent stall at the Walkers Market in North Mackay. It was always a family affair: me and my brother helping to set up, Mum helping with sales and handling the cash, and Dad displaying his weaving and wares.

As Dad progressed through these markets, he felt he had to take it to other towns, and that is what he did. While still running the stall at Walkers Market, he started travelling regularly to Airlie Beach Foreshore Market on a Saturday morning. The hordes of tourists bought his wares like hotcakes. Hats were especially popular, along with fruit baskets and fans. He also sold them ice-cold coconuts with straws and cocktail umbrellas. If he turned a good profit on a Saturday at Airlie Beach, we would travel through to Townsville's Flinders Street Market the following Sunday. Once again, the tourists would flock to buy everything he'd made during the week. At times, we'd travel further afield, to places like Winton, Gladstone, the Sunshine Coast, Rockhampton and even Darwin, to other markets, shows and arts festivals.

Dad had a network of fellow stallholders at the markets. They'd all trade wares, from leather goods to glass-blown ornaments, pottery, clothing and antiques. Our home was full of items from these market trades. Some of Dad's best artwork and artefacts are still in our family home today.

The demand never dried up for his cultural wares. He was approached numerous times by members of the public, asking for help with improvements to their homes or businesses, particularly with an Islander flair. He wove wall panels for local restaurants and houses, a roof for the fruit and veggie section at a local supermarket and large wall hangings of turtles, dugongs and sea birds for a hotel lobby. He was once approached by a woman who wanted him to weave a bikini for a swimsuit contest. Someone always wanted him to create something different.

Dad was also sought after for his cultural flare by local and interstate schools, TAFEs and events. He loved to teach and share his Torres Strait culture, educating children and teachers.

Dad received the nickname 'The Hatman' from a fellow stallholder at Airlie Beach, and it stuck. He then went corporate and had Hatman logos designed for T-shirts, signage and business cards. They featured a caricature of Dad and the motto 'Shading your head in North Queensland'. Market attendees soon knew who 'The Hatman' was, and he was on his way building a reputation in market circles.

After a few years, Oriama Ait Artefacts was turning a good profit and, with Dad busy with other cultural duties, he expanded.

In 1992, he employed two relatives as labourers. They supported him with such work as retrieving materials, helping him manufacture artefacts and preparing stock for weekend markets. Dad also purchased a large white Toyota Coaster bus from a relative in Bucasia. This bus was not only a family vehicle but also his travelling workshop. With an annex for the side of the bus, he could just pull up and set up his stall at markets and events. When he travelled to out-of-town markets, he would sleep in it for the night, taking refuge on the roof when it was too hot inside.

When Dad wasn't setting up at the markets, he'd be putting down numerous kup murris at parties and gatherings around Mackay. Over the years he was often called upon for this cultural knowledge. He always cooked the food to perfection, and his kup murris never failed him. I remember the first time he taught me how to set up a kup murri for a gathering at a school friend's house. Step by step he showed me, from the collecting of rocks and firewood to the wrapping of the food in banana leaves and hessian bags donated by the local supermarket. Not only did he imprint the process on me and my older brother, he liked to teach the hosts of the gatherings too.

Dad knew how to cook the Island way. From coconut rice to sop sop, fried scones, domboys, numus, blachan and fish soup. If he cooked too much, he'd share it with relatives. I was a below-standard student when it came to these Island recipes, but they are still instilled in my older brother, Juliean, today.

Some of my favourite recollections are of learning from Dad how to hunt and gather. Fishing was a customary practice and family activity. He taught my brother and me how to fish, collect bait and rig up a line, and we would go fishing all day. He taught us how to gather mussels, prawns and mud crabs from local creeks, how to make banana-leaf lures to catch Spanish mackerel off our local beach, and how to go trawling in our boat. Our deep freezer was always well stocked with fish.

Turtle hunting was a regular occurrence, right down to cleaning the shells. In those days, he taught us to use code when talking about it in public, as it was still illegal. Half the time I would get mixed up using the code words. Once a turtle was caught, he taught us never to be greedy with it and to share it out among the community, as in them days it was quite hard to obtain it. Sometimes Dad would go turtle hunting by himself. I would wake up asking, 'Mum, where's Dad?' After school, he would be in the backyard, cleaning the boat out and hiding the shell and turtle spear. I used to be curious and ask him, 'Where you been?', but he would speak to me in Island Creole so the neighbours could not understand. With that out of the way, he would hide the turtle shell on our chicken coop roof so that the green ants in the mango tree above would eat the remaining flesh out of the shell. One of the four shells we have today at our place in Bucasia was one he used to teach me, showing me how to clean it up and prepare it to hang on the wall.

He spoke to my brother and me constantly in Island Creole, talking to us in a way only we would understand, especially when you did not want non-Islanders to know what you were speaking about. We used nicknames for our in-laws. I could not understand why we were not to call them by their preferred names, but I was taught that you called your in-laws by nickname as this was the Islander way. Dad's nicknames for my uncles included 'Uncle Moonman' and 'Uncle Pigsy', and my Darwin relatives call my mum 'Aka Big Bus'. I thought it was funny, but this was just the norm for us.

We would often sit on our verandah at Bucasia in the evenings and Dad would play the guitar. Being self-taught and knowing how to read music, he was quite a musician, playing songs by the Eagles, John Lee Hooker and B.B. King. If we were not listening to him play the guitar he would tell us about his upbringing, stories from his working days in Western Australia on the railways and his travels around Australia as a young man. He introduced my brother and me to our first comic-book hero, the Phantom. To this day I still read Phantom comics and find that I relate to a lot of my Islander cousins through this comic.

Dad's comical Island nature meant every car and pet had a unique name, which made us different from non-Islanders. Our dog's name was No-friend because he was the only kelpie pup left at the pet store. Two of our Ford XC sedans were named Green Thunder and White Smoke because of their colour. Dad's late Uncle Clay had a fishing boat called *Captain America* because it had the American flag and colours painted on it. That was us as Torres Strait Islanders.

Having had only a limited formal education, Dad was very self-taught. He had many books on an array of topics, from history, geography and land rights to car mechanics. That was one thing he excelled at: fixing our car in the front yard. From oil changes to engine swaps, relying on neighbourly relatives and friends for help and always returning the favour. He knew he had to get the car up and running before the upcoming weekend market. I remember being inquisitive and learning as much as I could about cars, because I knew I would learn more about this when I got older.

Dad was liked by many in the community and taught me to be friendly to everyone. Being the person he was, he took people at face value. Local business owners, teachers and MPs always had time for him. Some of these people are still our family friends today. I carry his traits on today: be friendly, be happy, smile up and always have a laugh.

Unfortunately, Mum and Dad separated in mid-1994. He then lived with his relatives in Townsville and eventually settled down and from 1996 called Cairns home. He was still selling his cultural wares to international tourists, now on the Cairns Esplanade and using a new nickname, 'Friday'. When I visited him in my mid-teens, he was still pulling crowds and customers and turning a good profit to survive on.

With the markets still a part of his income, he continued to travel constantly between Port Douglas, Kuranda, Cairns and Townsville markets, and most weeknights he set up a street stall on Cairns Esplanade. He began working with a Cairns events company, not only hosting and liaising with corporate and promotional events, but even being called on to make sets for numerous movies such as *The Thin Red Line* and *The Island of Dr Moreau*.

The last time I saw Dad, in 1999, he was still on top of his game. He had asked me and my brother to visit for a few weeks as he needed help with a few jobs he was working on at the time. We helped produce wall hangings for a hotel lobby in Port Douglas, built an Islander hut for a festival in Mareeba and made cultural props for a corporate event.

Dad passed away on 5 August 2010. While mowing his lawn at his house in Cairns, he died of a sudden heart attack. I was fortunate enough to receive the last hats, fruit bowls and baskets he had made. The coconut fronds were still green when these woven items reached me in Victoria. From this observation, I knew he had still been going strong and doing what he did best, weaving.

When I think of Dad now, I think about what a big hole he left in the cultural landscape. With his passing, he took with him his unique knowledge of culture and lifestyle. I feel Dad was not recognised enough for his contribution to promoting Torres Strait Islander culture, and that is why I decided to submit to this book.

To this day, I am constantly reminded of my dad and the amazing effect he had on my life. His artefacts are in the main hallway of my house. They remind me of him whenever I walk out the front door. I owe my work ethic, skills and abilities to Dad. He taught me never to give up and to always keep striving forward, showing non-Islanders we can do it.

With the cultural knowledge I was taught, I constantly remind my son of who we are, where we come from and, especially, his grandfather's story. I am happy and proud to say that I am a Torres Strait Islander.

Having been taught from an early age about our connection to the sea, I retell this to my son today. No matter how far we live from 'san beach', the ocean will always be there for us, through good and tough times, even though we live three hours away. I impress on him that our loved ones who have passed away are there, and that sea, wind and water are them talking and healing us. I make sure we both travel at least three times a year to the beach, not only for recreation but to heal and connect.

When I visit the beach, Dad's spirit is always there, and when I see a town market, he'll always have a stall there, pulling the crowds.

## Cultured Pearl

### Jillian Boyd-Bowie

**Bloodlines**

*Wen yu luk neis serar i plai antap, san yumpla, ol Zagareb. Demtu*
*oltaim tok po wanenada. Demtu plai ai wan, antap dem nada wan.*

Translation: 'When you see the two terns flying high above
the others, that's us, the Zagareb. They always fly high above the
others, communicating with each other.'

I was sixteen when my mum told me that. I didn't understand what it truly meant until my journey of self-discovery
led me to where I am today, relationally, mentally, emotionally, spiritually and culturally. I believe it is the intrinsic part of
my bloodline that subconsciously drives me to achieve. It's in
my DNA.

I am Jillian Bowie. This is my story.

I am from the Samsep and Zagareb tribes of Erub and
Mer. My principal totems are the Neis Serar (two terns), Serar
(tern), Beizam (shark) and Nam (turtle). My wind is Ziai Wag,
the south-west wind. It is the short, variable season of shifting

winds that change from the Sager (south-easterly) to Naiger (north). Like our language, our totems represent a part of our geographical identity. They represent the animals and plants that are plentiful in the environment our tribes come from. I see them reflected throughout my life's journey; the characteristics of the animals in my grit, determination, efforts to help others and hunger to always strive to excel within the shifting seasons in pursuit of my purpose.

My father's heritage stems from the Boyd Clan of Ayrshire on the Firth of Clyde in Scotland. 'That's where the bit of milk in the coffee comes from,' I would say to others. My blood-lines also stem back to Parama Island in Papua New Guinea, to Malaya (now known as Malaysia) and to Lifou Island, part of the Loyalty Islands Province of New Caledonia. 'I am a tasty mix of tropical fruit salad with a dollop of cream' is another thing I say to people.


**Backdrop**

My childhood embraced everything Thursday Island repre-sents: a multicultural society built upon the influx of several ethnic groups that influenced our traditional dishes, our lan-guage, our appearance and our way of life.

I was born in 1970 on Thursday Island, traditionally known as Waibene, into an interracial marriage, which was not frowned upon because of the multiculturalism on Thursday Island (more affectionately known as TI to locals). TI had a mixture of Japanese, Chinese, Filipinos, Malayans, Melanesians, Pacific Islanders, Aboriginals and, of course, the British, Scots and Irish; and they all came with their religions, ideologies, cultures and recipes.

My white dad, the late David Boyd, was embraced by families as their 'Uncle Dave'. We knew very little about Dad's life, his personal or family history. He was a quiet, humble, intelligent man who didn't share much about his life and past experiences. When I became a mum, I made sure to find out more about my dad's history and family connections to pass on that knowledge to my children and grandchildren. Mum and Dad were well respected and well loved. They were hard workers and strong contributors to building our community, structurally and relationally.

My mother, the late Edith Tollie Boyd (née Sailor) of Erub and Mer, was a strong and proud Torres Strait Islander woman. She hailed from a family of hard workers whose fathers and uncles, through the progression of colonisation, would travel to faraway places on mainland Australia to find work with better pay to financially support their families. In the Torres Strait, they were used as cheap labour in industries based on rich local resources, such as pearls and bêche-de-mer (sea cucumbers), that foreigners were exploiting for the global market. In its newness, money became a commodity and a necessity, forcibly changing the lifestyle and culture of our people, who quickly learnt to walk in both worlds, one foot dancing to the drums of their cultural heartbeat and the other dangling in a foreign world in which they wanted to be acknowledged, accepted and treated as equals.

TI is a small, sheltered island, yet it is the most populated island in the Torres Strait because it serves as the administrative hub for the region and its eighteen island communities as well as two communities in the Northern Peninsula Area. When the British arrived, the government of the day segregated the lands into states and territories, and collectively labelled us

Aboriginal and Torres Strait Islanders. Torres Strait was annexed by Queensland in 1879, becoming part of the British colony. Before the Australian government's regionalisation of the country into states and territories, we identified ourselves according to our tribal space, referred to today as 'country' or 'ples'. To this day, colonisation has caused division between the two Indigenous groups of Australia now commonly known as Aboriginal and Torres Strait Islanders.

The Torres Strait Islands is an archipelago made up of mountain tops created by rising sea levels above what was once a land bridge between mainland Australia and Papua New Guinea over 10,000 years ago. We were and are very much a part of mainland Australia, with blood ancestry and language connections from Queensland and across to Northern Territory.

When our fathers, uncles and big brothers left home in the 1900s to find better-paid employment on the mainland, it left the women to run the households, raise the children, cultivate the gardens and work locally for low income in poor conditions.

My mother's primary school years came to an end when she was moved to Thursday Island to work as a 'nurse' and care for tuberculosis patients at the Aplin Hospital. I recall Mum telling me she had just reached puberty when the government pulled her out of school to work. Mum remained an employee of Queensland Health until she retired. Through six decades of earning minimal pounds and pennies, she would keep a small portion to survive and give the rest to her aging parents.

Mum and Dad were always happy. I had no idea, growing up, that our people were living under strict conditions, in a time of segregation, oppression and control. These conversations were not had around the dinner table. I was living in my own little bubble, unaware of what my mother had experienced, transitioning from the only life she knew into a foreign world, with little education and unclear of what was taking place and why.

I was born into this. It was normal for me to go to the open-air picture theatre and sit on canvas seats under the large tree, while non-Indigenous people sat upstairs on a veranda in comfortable seats and a roof that sheltered them from the rain. I was unaware that my mother was not allowed to enter the local pubs, that her education was limited to Year 7 or that there was a school for black students at the back of the island and a school for non-Indigenous students at the front. Apartheid was rife back then. Only a few years before, Mum's older brothers were only allowed to be educated up to Year 4. Among many other restrictions, the movements of our people – including where they could live, where they could travel and who they could marry – were controlled by Patrick Killoran, the 'Protector of Islanders'. Mum was once denied permission by Killoran to leave the island to visit her sister, who lived on another island, Mabuyag. So, Mum ran away as a stowaway, on a boat her brother worked on, to get there.

Mum was what we call a 'strong head', a stubborn black woman who did not like being controlled and was not afraid to use her voice. I am proud to have inherited my mother's strong traits, work ethic, resilience and courage.

## MATRIARCH

Soft grey skies, occupied poignant cries
of misplaced empresses in days gone by.

Revered powers burnt upon the woods over time, robbed
by [white] men with shaky hands and rickety legs starved in status
building disempowering systemic structures
to bury our shine.
To live beneath, and not by.

Woman come, sit with me upon our matrilineal throne
blameless bare bosoms mothering
souls stripped bare, uncovering spoils.

Deep calls unto deep lines through birdsongs
of ancient oracles.

Time travellers falling like rain from soft grey clouds
saturating sacred spaces of woman's business
sifting into warm hands of healers.

Knowledge holders outpouring
into the cusps of protectors
nurturing the famished into bellies full
and crowded minds.

Delivering newfound life into scriptures of old.

Drink your portion of historical nobility
a stolid state you dare not be.
To your role pledge fidelity.
Rest in your inheritance duly.
Welcome to your country.

## Childhood

Growing up as a child in the '70s on Thursday Island was different to growing up on the outer island communities. I did not have the privilege of speaking my mother's language because she did not speak it to us. We spoke Torres Strait Creole, now known as Yumplatok, and English as our second language. We learnt traditional dances and songs to perform at special events, we learnt how to cook traditional dishes and we practised customs such as fishing, hunting and gardening, which was more prevalent in some families than in others. We were not taught the truth in school about our people, language or history. We would sing nursery rhymes and songs about gory British historical events, oblivious to their origins and what they meant.

I attended the Catholic primary school, where Roman Catholicism was a mandatory part of the curriculum. However, Mum attended the Anglican church and would take us there every Sunday.

I spent my childhood and teenage years on TI creating lifelong friendships and strong kinship connections and enjoyed favourite pastimes savoured with salty plums, icy cups, fresh tamarinds and half-ripe mangoes marinated in Old Cathay soy sauce with a spoonful of sugar. Yum! After school, we would find ourselves at a friend's house playing the game of the season, whether that was skittles, marbles, snail fights, mud fights or boat races down the gushing gutters during monsoon season with our self-made boats … Time escaped us as we were engrossed in the thrill of the game. Still in school uniform, dusk would catch us unawares, and we would rush to get home before our parents, only to find them waiting to give us a hiding because we had not come straight home from school to do our chores.

Our chores would be making sure the kitchen sink was clean and the floors swept before our parents came home from work to cook dinner. We had to make sure our school uniforms were washed and hung up ready for the next day. Disobedience would bring a hiding, and the chores would move up a level to cleaning the windows and glass doors, and raking up the dried mango leaves in the yard and burning them in a heap. The smell of fire burning dry grass and leaves always connects me to home, family, fond memories and my identity.

The king tides during the festive season lured us children like the Pied Piper of Hamelin to swim all day, either at the beach, bomb-diving off the jetties, or playing tag, diving through the pristine green ocean surrounding the arched mangrove roots of Tamwoy Town. We would go home with eyes as red as the salty plums we ate, our skin shades a third darker than when we had left the house in the morning, and our wrinkled, white, pruney fingertips would dob us in. There were no crocodile problems back then on TI.

The boys would visit the local tip and collect parts to make corrugated-iron canoes to fill our afternoons with adventures, canoeing around the mangroves using disposed turtle shells as paddles. They would manufacture go-carts and makeshift bicycles to race down Stephen Street and up around Pilot Street like the Grand Prix on two wheels, with laid-back sunken seats and butterfly handles, like Harley Davidsons. We fished from a very young age, jigged sardines for bait and reeled in trevallies, mackerels, breams and many other species.

We had no TV until I was twelve years old, and there was only one channel at the time, the ABC. There were no mobile phones, iPads or internet back then. Our environment was our playground and our entertainment.

I lived at Tamwoy Town, a former reserve turned suburb at the back of TI. Previously known as Eagle Camp, Tamwoy Reserve was officially proclaimed on 9 February 1957. It is named after a respected leader and elder of Badu Island, the late Eccles Tamwoy. We eventually lived in a house my dad built, and that is where I spent my high school years. I loved high school. This is where my lifelong friendships were born, where close friends became family. They became my brothers and sisters, uncles and aunties to my children, and grandparents to my grandchildren. These are the valued extended family kinship embraced through relationship. It is not only blood nor kin that defines 'family' in Indigenous cultures. It is the strong bond of love, trust and relationship that defines family.

I excelled in sports, and English was my favourite subject at school because I loved to write. I love learning new words, the power of words and how they can be constructed to help people escape their realities, create new ones, evoke emotions, provoke thoughts and empower those who accept its strength.

### Barefoot in a concrete jungle

After graduating high school in 1987, I moved to mainland Australia, as young Torres Strait adventurers do. I craved new experiences and wanted to meet new people. I had no vision, no dreams, no purpose. No one mentored me or gave me direction in life. These were not discussions my parents or uncles and aunties had with me. Life itself was my teacher, my mentor and the firm hand that disciplined me as I followed the urges of my heart. I learned everything the hard way and on my own. I became a young mum four months before my twenty-first birthday. Over the course of fifteen years, I had six children and two failed relationships, worked several different jobs, faced many challenges and low points.

Over the course of time, I started my spiritual and cultural journey of healing and self-discovery. It was through the tough times in life that I acquired my ever-growing strength and wisdom. Through trial and error, and my willingness to humble myself, to listen and learn from everything that surrounds me.

I was determined to pass on to my children everything I learnt and give them what I never had from my parents, attentive love and guidance. My parents were very strict and 'old school'. They demonstrated their love in ways of providing food, shelter and discipline. I wanted my children to experience tangible love, and to impart to them a sense of pride and respect for who they are, and to empower them as individuals into their calling. I wanted to raise my sons as strong yet humble and respectful young men who treat women with love and respect, and work hard to support their families. I wanted to raise my daughters to become virtuous women, strong pillars in their households and their communities; I wanted them to learn from my mistakes and strive to be better than the woman I had become. Each generation should be stronger and wiser than the last, learning from past mistakes and successes to adapt to the times. More importantly, I wanted my children to be happy, healthy and safe in life.

I lived on mainland Australia for over thirty years before I moved back home to the Torres Strait. Living in a few different cities introduced me to racism, systemic discrimination and stereotyping. I lived through toxic relationships, domestic violence, drug and alcohol abuse. I was no longer living in the protective bubble of my parent's care, and was exposed to the harsh realities of the nation we live in.

I learnt about what 'white privilege' meant, and more and more about our political history and the injustices placed on First Nations people. I learnt about the White Australia policy and attempts to outbreed the blacks. I learnt about the Stolen Generation, stolen wages and stolen lands. I learnt about derogative terms that we took and adopted into our own language, like 'half-castes', 'piccaninnies' and 'Aboriginal', according to Uncle Colin Jones, Kalkadoon and Nunukul elder, scholar, and lecturer in Aboriginal culture, art and history.

## Adding milk to my coffee

Growing up as a Torres Strait Islander on TI, I never saw myself as an 'outsider' because of my brown skin, and I was never treated as one, because of the island's cultural diversity and my mother's family status and heritage. I was about forty-five years old when the breakthrough of my decade-long contemplation became my reality. I was fifty per cent white and had never connected to the other half of my identity, which had blessed me with inherent traits I take for granted. Although I was half white, I would never be seen or accepted as white; nor did I identify as a white person. I was fully embraced as a Torres Strait Islander, accepted and loved by Torres Strait Islanders and seen as an Indigenous woman. That to me speaks volumes about what differentiates the two races.

For quite some time, I had been thinking about connecting with my dad's side of the family, not knowing what to expect, whether or not I would be accepted, because I was Indigenous. I had gotten to know my dad's two sisters growing up, and they were lovely and accepting. They continued to write to Mum after Dad passed in 1992. I had met two of my dad's brothers when Dad was in hospital with cancer. I just wasn't sure about my white cousins, nephews and nieces living abroad. Doubts like these emerged after my move to mainland Australia and the experiences I endured there. However, the past decade has connected me with a few of my beautiful family members, and I am learning more about the Boyd family history as the years pass by.

## Growth

It was not easy being a single mum of six children with no physical or financial support from anyone. I had amazing friends who were always there for moral support and in a time or two of crisis, but mostly I felt alone in my struggles. It was difficult for me to ask for help or accept it. Yet, through each predicament, I pulled through for my children; and each time I conquered a circumstance, I added another feather to my wings.

Other mums would say to me, 'I don't know how you do it with six. I struggle with my two!'

I always say to them, 'You don't know the strength a single mother possesses until she is faced with a circumstance where her children's survival depends on it. Like a Mama Bear protecting her cubs, it becomes second nature.'

### EVERYDAY HERO

Silent years masquerade purpose
An empty cup overflows
Unpleasant moments blemish life, love.

Silent tears saturate a hero's cape
Flowing unwillingly from sweaty nape
In bleak secret spaces, healing cries beckon hope.
Future stretches its arms back in time
Its flirtatious fingers successful in rescue
A lean soul rises from darkened depths
Whispering to the dawning strength of human spirit.

Out of mourning,
warnings of failures echo its drownings
The awakening dawn disturbs precious slumber
The everyday hero meets another first step.

## Passion to purpose

Today, I am a wife and mother, a grandmother and mentor, a writer and poet, a business owner and contributing community member. I am everything I can be right now and happy in my space. Everything I do is with purpose ... We all have a purpose. We belong to something bigger than ourselves. Otherwise, why are we here?

As I matured in life, my cultural lens seasoned with me. I am one small part of a tiny nation many have not heard about. For me, living as a Torres Strait Islander comes with expectations: to understand what it means to be a sovereign people, the custodians of our lands, seas, culture and language; to trust that we have successfully governed ourselves and maintained our environment for thousands of years and can continue to do so.

We must encourage and empower our youth, our future leaders, to get educated, to learn more about our people, our history, our languages, culture and purpose, otherwise it will all fade away, along with our identity and sovereign rights. This begins in our homes and filters out into the lives and hearts of others to acknowledge and accept.

Our ancestors fought for equality, justice and the freedom to live *our* way, to make our own decisions according to our lore and governance, and to decide what that would look like in this twenty-first century. We are our own people, and it is our sovereign right to have that freedom. Our ancestors left a burning torch for us to pick up, to help us strive towards the vision, because we are not there yet. This became my purpose. I picked up the torch in my forties when the sudden urgency of this vision burned in my spirit. But I had to go through my own transformational journey first. I had to find myself beneath all the layers of complexities and influences that suffocated my true self and my personal truths. I accepted that all the influences, good and bad, created the woman I am today, and I learned how to harness my strengths and to travel with my identity and purpose.

My foundation must be strong before I can help others. I listen, I learn, I read and I put into action effective strategies to take control of my life, rather than life controlling me. I soon became a transformational coach and mentor, helping others to discover themselves and their purpose.

Every day counts for me, because I started this journey late in life and see the urgency of addressing the issues my people face. I don't like wasting time, our most precious commodity, at such a critical season … We must take control of the governance of our people and the protection of our homelands. There must be an added focus to our dinner-table conversations and our school curricula, and a strong push to upskill, educate and empower our people. This is a necessary foundation for the construction of self-governance and self-sustainability.

Knowledge is power, but it is useless if it is not used to benefit our purpose. We must add feet to our faith, hands to our understanding and keep our minds clear and focused.

What do our ancestors expect from us?

What would we, when we become ancestors, expect from our future generations?

## DESCENDANT

My voice echoes the cries of my forefathers
My feet trek truths of my ancestors
I rise in the essence of my predecessors
In pursuit of visions once dreamt

### Faith to freedom

Christianity was introduced to our people on 1 July 1871, known as 'The Coming of the Light', which from my perspective was done in the most culturally inappropriate way possible by the London Missionary Society (LMS). Nonetheless, it has influenced our spiritual beliefs and customs as a people because we could relate to a 'creation spirit' and an 'evil spirit' and had lores similar to the Ten Commandments. That demonstrates that we were already connected to the spiritual realm long before the LMS. As a Torres Strait Islander Christian today, I embrace both my Christianity and my culture as part of my identity and what I stand for. My spiritual lens opened through my journey of self-discovery and influenced my perception on some religious practices and interpretations of who God is and what God represents. Growing in my spirituality meant addressing man-made theologies and religious attitudes that had indoctrinated our people, causing division and loss of culture.

Spirituality for me is simple. It's about believing in God and growing in one's relationship with Him, without negating our identity in Christ or cultural identity, nor creating idols that replace God in our lives, whatever that idol represents; whether it be money, lust, materialism or culture itself. It's about practising good, not evil, whether within the cultural space or not. The LMS preached that our cultural practices were evil and believed they came to 'civilise the savages', expecting us to deny our identity, language and customs in the process. Every culture, black or white, has evil practices. When I discovered that many Indigenous and ethnic cultures around the world had similar beliefs about spirituality, creation and the afterlife, I concluded that we all believe in something and a Creator greater than ourselves, and we all label them differently, according to our environment and cultural understanding. To each their own. Life is a journey of growth, physically, mentally and spiritually. We will never know everything about life beyond our physical space until we get there. I believe I am spirit first, before my decaying flesh and bones. In that, I build my strong foundation and surety, knowing that all else in life will follow suit.

It is the goodness in my life that gives me strength, hope, balance and keeps my spirit alive; my children and grandchildren, my friends, my marriage, my work, my God. I live and breathe my purpose, treading carefully so as not to bring pain and suffering but love and empowerment to a people I am proud and privileged to be a part of.

# JOURNEY

To what do I owe the pleasure, of this next breath taken?
To the fresh scent of wet earth, the morning rain is creatin?
To the glorious sight of pink desert rose frolicking in heaven's dew?
To the sound of distant thunder grumbling out of misty blue?

I pondered and panged on the eve of my dawn
Awakening translated in the light of morn
Dying to self since Journey was born
A hangover effect like ex lover's scorn.

She introduced me to life, love, to pain inhumane
Clothed in content, contempt, still hope kept me sane
Desires dreamt, as sure fire remained
I know now that to lose means to gain.

Showers of sorrows, madness, and rages
Stabbed in the dark on blood-stained pages.
A wounded bird, with broken wings
Since beautiful morphed from broken things.

Yet unafraid to fly, to make best and try
Continue the climb to my place of rest.
Journey's voice trembled on eggshells at first
Then roars of a lion, quenched its thirst.

Magnificent monuments built over time
Memory by memory, line upon line
Influenced fragments merged into one
Seasoned, as spice and sugars run.

In bloodline's savour as taste on my tongue
The hard work of sufferings undeniably done.

I dwell in the sweetness of my mountaintop's cleft
With a view to die for with what life I have left.
Thank God each morning for another breath
As each day draws near to another death.

We live and learn without discern
As predestined moments take Journey's turns
The good and the bad behind labelled faces
Too many to count, the Jacks, Jokers, and Aces.

Still I rise as Queen of my kingdom,
Straighten my crown from the qualms I evolved from
Truth is a gift as justice sustains me.
That set me and kept me, free in my journey.

I move like the wind, freely and swiftly
Amid cracks and crevices dare to inform me
Across treetops and grand hills escaping realities
Then into the valleys in familiar territories.
To ride the waves high through stormy seas
Disrupting the calm of complacencies
Grand gestures waving from perfectionists' dreams
To awaken giants from wallowing reams.

Pillows drenched with wildfire dreams,
Suffocating stains of inaccuracies
Then comes words, purposed and necessary
Creating magic, recording memories.

I know enough to live what I know
She taught me forgiveness to unanchored soul.

Flourished in dreams and other's esteems.
Strengthened by scorns and futile mockery.

Far have I travelled from those who betrayed me.
Scars and wounds kept close to remind me.
Of Journey, creatively shaping destiny.
Not to prove others wrongly,
but believe in myself, conclusively.

# My Island Home and Away

**Ellen Armstrong**

The strong yearning for my cultural heritage is calling me now that I have lost my Nana Suko, my great-grandmother.

Every night when I would visit her in Mackay, we would sit down and watch *Home and Away* along with my grandmother, Nana Rhonda. This was a ritual for us, and as a child I didn't care for it much. But now that Nana Suko is gone, I miss these moments, and I am still looking for the connection I have lost. I don't seem to understand why *Home and Away* was such an important show to both Nana Suko and Nana Rhonda. Was it the drama-filled relationships or the outrageous storylines? Whatever it was, it was essential viewing, and every night they would stop everything to watch it.

Newcastle, Mulubinba, in Awabakal Country, is my home. My name is Ellen, and my family is from Boigu Island, Queensland, but I was born and raised in Newcastle, New South Wales. I lived with my mother, Leah, my father, Warwick, and my younger brother, Wessley. My mother was born and raised in Mackay, and that is where my Island family lives. Growing up in Newcastle meant I wasn't around a lot of Torres Strait Island culture, but I grew up being part of the Aboriginal community. In school, my brother and I took part in Aboriginal dancing and activities as there were no other Torres Strait Islander kids around. We would march every NAIDOC Week with the Aboriginal community and do all the Aboriginal activities. Regardless, Mum raised us to be proud Torres Strait Islanders. We would wear the Torres Strait flag to all the events and always ensured people knew we were Torres Strait Islander because we were proud of our heritage.

When Nana Suko and Nana Rhonda came to Newcastle to visit, they would always bring Island food like mud crabs, fish, prawns and dugong. If it was the right season, they would also bring frozen mangoes and Dad would make smoothies. Mum, Nana Suko and Nana Rhonda would spend hours in the kitchen cooking up the food, singing, dancing, laughing and sharing stories of their childhoods. I would sit and watch them. My favourite food was mud crab. I always wanted the biggest claw, and there was always a fight over who could have it. It usually ended with Dad getting it. When Nana Suko and Nana Rhonda visited, we always asked Aunty Ettie (who lived in Sydney, Dharug Country) to come up and stay with us. Her laughter would always make me giggle. She was big and boisterous, and once you got her going the whole house would be in tears from laughter. She and Nana Rhonda grew up together and were like sisters. I remember one year Nana Suko made a grass hula skirt for me and taught me how to Island dance. All four ladies would be up and shaking their hips like they were in their twenties again, and I would try to keep up. Then 7 p.m. would roll around and there we would be, sitting in front of the TV, everyone focused on *Home and Away*.

Mackay, Yuwi Country, is my home away. Every school holidays I would go and visit Nana Suko and Nana Rhonda. Sometimes by myself, other times with my brother. Mum and Dad would take us to the airport, check us in, hand us over to the flight attendants and send us on our way. One time, they forgot to request an escort for us for our four-hour stopover in Brisbane. No problem for me. I was a determined seven-year-old who took us straight to the gate, and we sat there until our flight was ready. I had been flying to and from Mackay since I was three.

When we arrived in Mackay, Nana Rhonda would be there to pick us up at the airport, and we would stay with her and my uncle. Fishing, crabbing, running through the mangroves and along the beach were how we spent our holidays. When I was four, Nana Suko taught me how to scale a fish, cut it open and remove all the guts. When fishing, I was never allowed to use a rod, I always had to make sure it was a handline, even though I was no good and hated using the handline. Nana Rhonda would take me out into the mangroves with a long stick and show me how to poke around, looking for uckles (mussels). Nana Suko and Nana Rhonda are my connection to my Island identity. Both nanas made sure I knew where we came from and who we were. They are my idols. Whenever we went to visit, I always wanted to be near them and to listen to their stories of how they grew up.

Sadly, Nana Suko passed in 2020 at the young age of 103. She was an amazing woman. Still fishing well into her late nineties, always joking around, she loved a good yarn. One of the last things I remember her telling me was 'You don't need no man, all they do is take all your money.' She was one of the last connections I had to the Island.

Nana Suko was removed from the Islands during World War II. The government was concerned she could become a spy for the Japanese. You see, in 1936, she had a relationship with a Japanese pearl-shell diver and had a child (Nana Rhonda). When the war started, he returned to Japan to serve in the war in China, and Nana Suko was forced to move down to a mission in Cherbourg. The Japanese man never returned to Australia. Nana Suko then moved to Mackay, where she met my Poppy, Ram Chandra. Ram Chandra was an Indian snake handler, also known as the Taipan Man. Nana Suko and Poppy married and had eight children together. They both stayed in Mackay until they passed. I was five when Poppy passed and twenty-seven when Nana Suko passed. I loved both Nana Suko and Poppy so much. I always make sure to go and visit them at the cemetery.

For me, self-expression comes out in tattoos. I have a tattoo on my right foot for Poppy. The tattoo is of a shell. When I was a toddler, Poppy and I were walking along the beach and he found this beautiful shell. Of course, being so young, I wanted it. Poppy said it was our special shell and kept it at their house for me, so I could see it every time I came up. When he passed, I superglued it onto his tombstone. Unfortunately, a few years later it was stolen. So, when I turned eighteen, it was my first tattoo. My parents were not happy about this, but as soon as I showed Nana Suko she started crying and touching it, saying, 'Oh, that's Ellen and Poppy's special shell'. On my left foot is Nana Suko's favourite flower, a frangipani, and surrounding the frangipani is our Island totem, the Dhoeybaw (big heart vine). I feel them walking through life with me, watching over me and guiding me to find out who I am and to connect back to culture.

Nana Rhonda is more like a mother to me than a grandmother. She helped raise my brother and me when my parents were working and travelling. Each year she would come and stay at least three months in Newcastle with us. She taught me how to make numus (pickled fish) and damper. She would show me old photos of her life growing up and tell me stories about Nana Suko and Poppy. In Mackay, we would drive around looking for mangos and lychees on the trees and quicky grab them before anyone caught us. When I visit today, we still cruise around the town, scoping out the trees for hidden treats. The time I spend with Nana Rhonda I cherish the most.

The Torres Strait Islands is where I feel at home when I am away from home. When I was four years old, I made my first trip to the Islands. Unfortunately, as I was young, I don't remember much. In 2020, I asked Nana Rhonda to take me for my twenty-seventh birthday. Since the passing of Nana Suko, I had felt a gap in my life that was yearning to be filled with culture. Nana Rhonda and I went up and stayed with an aunty on Horn Island. As soon as I stepped off the plane, I felt the heat. I had chosen to go just at the start of summer and my body was not ready for it. A cousin took me to watch the footy finals that were taking place on Thursday Island and drove me around. As I stood at the top of the hill, looking out over the island, I realised how different my life was on the mainland and in Newcastle. The Islands are a completely different world to what I have known most of my life.

We went over to Prince of Wales Island in a dinghy. The seas were a bit rough, and we were thrown around a bit, but I loved every moment of it. I was just so happy to be there. We stayed with Aunty Lala and Uncle Joe. They lived in this big house on top of the hill with electricity supplied by a generator, surrounded by cats and dogs. Aunty Lala took Nana Rhonda and me around the island in this little old Suzuki four-wheel drive that broke down multiple times throughout the trip. I sat in the water, ensuring I kept my eyes peeled for crocs, as I was petrified. Aunty Lala wanted some seedpods to made kulups (rattles) and jewellery, so we took an adventure into the bush. Imagine seeing two small Island women and one tall white Island girl running around in the bush with huge sticks, trying to get the seedpods off the trees.

Nana Rhonda got a cake made for my birthday and ensured there was dugong for me to eat. We went out to Friday Island for a special meal at Kazu Pearl Farm, where my aunty Rhonda is a part owner. This trip was exactly what I needed to feel connected to Nana Suko and my Island culture. Feeling the water and walking along the land gave me such a strong sense of who I was. Even though I came back red from too much sun, I knew that the trip with Nana Rhonda meant as much to her as it did to me.

And now here I am. Living in Brisbane, Meeanjin, in Turrabul Country, halfway between home and home away. I am still on my cultural journey. Still trying to fill the hole in my heart left by Nana Suko. Along this journey I have learnt to accept who I am, a fair-skinned Island woman. There are many times when I have questioned my cultural identity, being told I was 'too white' or that 'you can't be Torres Strait Islander, you didn't grow up there'. The most important thing I tell myself is that no one can take it away from me. I know who my family is, and even though I didn't grow up on the Islands, that doesn't make me any less of a Torres Strait Islander. My connection to my family and culture is still strong and will continue to grow as I grow.

## Lessons from My Grandmother: A Window to the World

### Leilani Bin-Juda

'You not only belong to us in the Torres Strait; you belong to the world' —Elder Aunty Flo Kennedy, 2009

My name is Leilani Bin-Juda. I am a proud Torres Strait Islander with Hammond, Darnley and Murray Islands heritage. My ancestors also came from different countries throughout Asia and the Pacific. Having such a rich and diverse Indigenous and multicultural background, I have had an extraordinary life with amazing adventures, personally and professionally. *Growing Up Torres Strait Islander in Australia* provides an opportunity to share my journey.

The Torres Strait is a group of islands situated between the tip of North Queensland and Papua New Guinea's Western Province. We are a unique group of people as Torres Strait Islanders, with shared cultural values, respect and kastom. While we are a small population, we have constructively contributed (and continue to contribute) to regional, domestic and international affairs.

Queensland is the only Australian state or territory which shares a border with a foreign country – Papua New Guinea. The Torres Strait Treaty between Australia and Papua New Guinea, signed in 1978 and enacted in 1985, permits the cross-border movement of traditional inhabitants freely within the Torres Strait Protected Zone. This treaty is one of a kind in international law. It exists because of our strong traditional ties and the vision of our forefathers to ensure that our traditional way of life and livelihoods would be maintained. I have had an extensive and intimate knowledge of the implementation of the treaty, as I will expand on later.

The Torres Strait is best known for its fishing and pearling industries, which continue today. It is also a strategic location for defence and security. Importantly, we maintain our rich music, art and culture. Our most significant legal milestone was the High Court's *Mabo* decision on 3 June 1992, which challenged the notion of terra nullius, or land belonging to no one. In the landmark decision, our unique rights to land and sea were recognised as native title. It was a huge achievement.

My people are expert navigators, adventurers, innovators, ambassadors, teachers, storytellers, performers, strategists, chefs and advocates for change. The blood runs deep when I reflect on the past and present, and imagine what our future might look like. This is my story of growing up Torres Strait Islander, filled with good yarns which have inspired and challenged the person I am now, and the person I continue to become.

## Early life

I was born in Cairns in 1974, the first daughter, with three older brothers. Four years later, my younger sister was born. Being the first daughter was a blessing and a challenge, as I came to realise a bit later, in my teens. These formative years influenced my drive for social justice and gender equality.

My maternal grandmother, Phyllis Lillian Hodges (née Savage), had a huge influence on my life, both then and now. In my earliest memory, aged four, I can remember Granny getting me ready for a road trip. We were driving to Gladstone in her fawn-coloured Holden Belmont to visit her cousin, Grandad Pedro Guivarra, and his family.

I grew up with lots of cousins, but my favourite place was Granny's. Grandchildren, nieces and nephews gravitated to her house – on Cavallaro Avenue in Cairns – especially the boys, as she always had a pot of something on the stove and they were huge eaters! Often she would say, 'Pile your plate like Naghi' – an island in the Torres Strait known for its distinctive peak. Food is everything to us. Granny came from humble beginnings and was a strong lady, hardworking, a straight shooter, a larrikin and very funny. A sense of humour is a common family trait!

She ensured we knew our family heritage and culture. While her family moved from Darnley Island to Cairns in search of employment, Granny took every opportunity to share stories, songs and culture with us. When we went to funerals, especially in the Anglican church, she would sing Island hymns, and I would look up at her and think how amazing she was. She had a fantastic voice and would always sing 'How Great Thou Art'. Often, she would burst out singing a rendition of 'Pearly Shells' or 'Sweet Leilani', which as a kid I found a bit embarrassing, but later in life I treasured these moments the most. When I wasn't with her, I would often call her on the telephone to check on her. To this day, her telephone number is firmly imprinted in my brain. Funnily enough, I cannot remember anyone else's number but hers.

Now and then, on her gramophone, Granny would play the Fijian song 'Isa Lei'. The Pacific and Island music was never far from her thoughts. There was always music, card games and lots of cigarette smoke in her house. Granny was a chain smoker. We would complain, but she would tell us to 'just breathe out the window' – yes, a straight shooter! Interestingly, none of her grandchildren smoke, but we are fiercely competitive when playing cards, board games, sports or just about anything. I think this streak came from her. Us kids would be around the table most days, trying to cheat her cards out of her hand when she wasn't looking.

Granny was also our babysitter and would often collect me and my younger siblings (including my cousin brother Benjamin Hodges) in her little white Daihatsu bus (rainbow sticker on the side) from our Catholic primary school, armed with hot chips and potato scallops, or there would be a courtesy trip to Johnson's Super Mart on Mulgrave Road for treats. This is where I learned about the 'book up', or line of credit.

Granny had an account with Johnson's and with the local butchery. On pay day, she would settle the accounts. I came to realise that her seasonal work at Queerah meatworks was irregular and she would find other ways to supplement her income. One of those was one of her favourite pastimes – playing bingo. My younger siblings and I could often be found with her at the bingo halls on school holidays and weekends, keeping her company and playing one or two little tickets. Sometimes we might be allowed to go with her on school nights, but that was rare.

Christmas time was always fun and revolved around food. All the favourite Island dishes would be on offer. This included her sensational sop sop, a traditional dish made with taro, yam, pumpkin, banana and sometimes chicken. The vegetables would be covered in freshly squeezed coconut milk and encased in the banana leaf in a saucepan. The creek at the back of Granny's house served as her taro plantation. I always tried to be at Granny's early, so that I could watch her prepare. She'd start by issuing orders to her brother Edward to cut the banana leaf and scrape the coconuts. Then she'd burn the banana leaf on the gas stove. I loved those moments, watching her cook as she talked to me.

Then Granny got a job as a cook at the local Warringu Aboriginal Women's Shelter. One day we were sitting at the table, big cups of tea in hand, and Granny told me she wanted my help. I was probably in my early teens at the time. She'd been asked to give a talk to the clients at the shelter about her life. It was through this process that she shared how hard her life had been – chopping wood to make fire, standing in the sun when she was a kid to keep warm, her family making food stretch as best they could and sometimes going hungry when there wasn't anything. She told me to study hard, as education was the key to a better life. These were sentiments I have always held strongly, then and today.

**Teen years**

When I was ten, life started changing. It became apparent to me that there were very clear divisions of work based on gender. Boys did garden chores and could go wherever they liked, but girls stayed in the house to clean and serve. As the first daughter, this was a hard pill to swallow. It ignited a sense of social justice and equality within me, as well as a fierce need for independence.

A few years later, relatives started a hula dance group, and we had to attend dance practice and perform at family cultural events. These performances, where we would dress in frangipani leis and raffia skirts, were both exciting and embarrassing as a teenager. Thinking about body image and being in front of an audience were things I did not enjoy.

It wasn't until Granny's sister (Holly Savage) had her tombstone unveiling that things started to click for me. This time, we practised traditional Torres Strait Islander dance. I loved it because Granny would make sure everyone listened to the strict instructions of our teacher, Mr Sambo. We paid particular attention to our posture and how we carried ourselves. Now this I could relate to. It was discipline and cultural learning. Those early experiences and Granny's influence formed strong foundations which have shaped me. I have come to learn that life is an evolving journey, not a linear progression.

## Schooling

I enjoyed going to high school in Cairns, and I was a good student. I had lots of cousins, including Peter Pilot and young Holly Savage, and a good set of friends.

My father was a seaman and worked on the boats all his life, as did his father, brother, cousins and uncles. This meant that in the 1980s, when I was about fifteen, we moved from Cairns to Weipa, on the west coast of Cape York. Some weekends we would visit relatives further north, at Mapoon. Aunty Gina and Uncle Silva Blanco and the old woodfired oven with damper cooking are fond memories.

In Weipa, I started working after school as a Woolworths checkout operator when I was fourteen years old. Work ethics ran deep in my family and so did understanding the value of the dollar. On one side of the family were business people with strict money values, the other side of the family lived pay week to pay week, but as long as they had a good time nothing else mattered.

I attended the local Weipa high school for six months, but the curriculum was limited. The temperature would soar to forty degrees and there was no air-conditioning in the class-rooms. Quite often I would come home for lunch, complain that the heat was too much and abscond in the afternoon. I aspired to further study, so eventually I returned to Cairns for schooling.

Back in Cairns, I stayed at the Joe McGinness Hostel, a facility for Aboriginal and Torres Strait Islander high school students from remote communities. There were about twenty other kids from the Torres Strait and Cape York, and we boarded at the hostel with our house parents, Jan and Jeff Wenitong. The hostel was named after an extraordinary Aboriginal activist who advocated for political and social justice.

Schooling was both challenging and rewarding. When allowed out on weekends, I would stay with Granny. Her sister Ivy and Granny's first husband, Noel Hodges Snr, lived on the same street as the hostel. Sometimes, in the afternoons, I would walk down to talk with Granny Ivy and listen to her stories about growing up on Darnley Island. She told me that when her family first moved to Cairns, they did not speak a word of

English, only the traditional language of Meriam Mir. I thought that was extraordinary. In one generation we had lost our ability to speak our mother tongue fluently. This was, of course, a reflection of government policy at the time, and Elders were forbidden to speak traditional languages.

In my senior year of high school, aged seventeen, I was volunteered by the hostel's house parent, Jan, and by my mother, to enter the regional Miss NAIDOC competition. Given my fear of public appearances at such a vulnerable age, I tried every form of resistance. All were unsuccessful. I was bundled off to the registration, where I met twenty other young hopefuls.

I didn't care about the outcome of the competition until my cousin and fellow contestant Chlor Fatnowna told me a story. One of the other girls had announced that because she was pretty and thin, she would win, so the rest of us really shouldn't bother. Clearly, this had upset my cousin, and at that moment, perhaps my drive for social justice came to the surface, or perhaps just plain family competitiveness arose. I told Chlor that we would give this thing a 'good bloody go'. I would not let my cousin be torn down or any of the other young girls be made to feel less than. My game face was on!

As Indigenous Australians, competition is unnatural to us. We have communal values and a strong sharing culture, deeply embedded in respect and reciprocity. But we can adapt to the circumstances when we need to. This is explored more in my work experience, a bit later on.

There were NAIDOC events all week, including recorded interviews to test our public presence, culminating in the NAIDOC Ball on the final night. My fellow students at the hostel wished me well for the big night. As the car taking me to the ball drew away, I felt very connected, because I was representing all of us who came from remote communities and our struggles just to be there.

Dressed in a pink organza gown of my own design (and matching heels), I ripped my dress before I went on stage. This is what happens when you're a simple kid and have never worn heels before! Jan panicked, but then she fixed it. I rehearsed my answer to the question the MC might ask – what does NAIDOC mean to you? – and then it was my turn to go on stage. My family was in the audience, including Granny.

Later, I stood next to Chlor as we waited for the winner to be announced. We were all giggling and laughing, until I realised – it was my name! I turned to Chlor and said, 'This is for you – it's more than beauty, it's brains.' We hugged each other, and I knew then that my life would be about advocacy, about proving naysayers wrong and fighting for justice. I went on to win a typing competition and a secretarial award at school the same year. My competitive streak started to grow.

## What do you want to be when you grow up?

When I was a kid, I would test my younger sister by teaching her the ABCs. I was a very strict instructor, and as I neared the end of high school, I wanted to study to be a teacher. But Dad said, 'No, there's no money in that.' I announced that I would join the Navy instead. This riled Dad up, and he replied, 'The Navy is no place for a girl.' This again raised the question of gender equality. Why couldn't I work on boats like my brother Shayne did? He went to the Australian Maritime College in Tasmania and was travelling everywhere as a young man. I wanted to do the same – where were my equal rights? Eventually, Dad and I agreed that I would study business, and that I could do whatever I wanted afterwards.

I respected my father immensely and would never defy him. His influence played a key role in my love of boats and fishing.

I commenced a degree in business studies at Central Queensland University in Rockhampton. Rockhampton was not as big as Brisbane, but far away from my parents and family, finally, I could be independent. I met my cousin Jenon Raymond, and my dear friend Ishani Kumarasinghe, who is of Sri Lankan heritage. We became the best of buddies and remain so even to this day. At university, I met many students from different countries and developed a deep connection to travel, culture and adventure.

In my second year of university, I moved into a shared villa with two Indonesians and a New Caledonian. We were in House 3. The Fijian Indians were in House 1, and the Solomon Islanders were in House 2. Each fortnight, we assembled in our common driveway and had a huge barbeque. I loved their food – chicken tandoori and curry, satay and nasi goreng. They were the flavours of the world and reminded me of home.

I managed to travel to New Caledonia when I was nineteen years old. I spent six amazing weeks travelling from the south to the north of the island. It was my first overseas experience, and I was hooked by adventure, by the beauty of the country and its people, and by the amazing fusion of Pacific and French food. Little did I know then the impact it would have on my life.

## Canberra connection – the public service

After university, I landed a graduate job in Canberra, working in the Australian Public Service for what was then the Department of Primary Industries and Energy. I commenced my duties on 6 February 1995. The date was significant – New

Zealand's Waitangi Day. Living in Canberra back then was hard. The weather was cold and miserable during winter, and I was a long way from home. But I loved the Canberra Raiders rugby league team, and that was a key factor in my decision to move to the nation's capital to begin with.

I met up with a few other Torres Strait Islanders, including my cousins Kay and Holly Savage, also from Cairns, and Destiny Devow, whose grandmother had knocked around with my grandmother's twin sisters. They had already been living and working in Canberra for years. I figured that if they'd been there so long it couldn't be that bad, and maybe I should try it. It was a great time when another cousin, Julie-Ann Guivarra (Grandad Pedro's granddaughter), also came to Canberra. She worked for the Department of Foreign Affairs and Trade as a graduate and would later become a senior executive.

For some time, the Canberra-based Torres Strait Islanders wanted to form a Torres Strait Islanders corporation. It would enable us to bring everyone together, undertake activities to keep culture strong and access funding for community development. We formed the first ACT Torres Strait Islanders Corporation thanks to a few key founding members doing the heavy lifting – in particular Destiny Devow and Della Cornforth. Both Destiny and Della worked in the Office of the Registrar of Indigenous Corporations and were expert in the establishment of corporations and the relevant legislation. Elections were held, and I was elected as the chairperson at the corporation's inaugural meeting – the youngest chairperson of any corporation under the *Aboriginal and Torres Strait Islander Corporations Act*. The corporation continues today.

Canberra also provided other career opportunities. Having worked in various government agencies, by chance I was asked to undertake project work at the National Museum of Australia for the Torres Strait Islander gallery space, in the lead-up to the 2001 opening of the museum's new building on the Acton Peninsula. At first, I didn't even know what a museum was! Our museum is a living environment, not a static building with treasures inside. There were a handful of us Indigenous curators at the time, in the Aboriginal and Torres Strait Islander Program.

My first task at the museum was to escort a group of Torres Strait Elders to the United Kingdom. We visited Cambridge University Museum of Archaeology and Anthropology (CUMAA) to select cultural objects for the National Museum of Australia's opening exhibitions. CUMAA holds the oldest recorded Torres Strait historical collection in the world – the nineteenth-century Haddon Collection. The project was exciting, emotionally charged and hard work. The exhibition we curated was part of the First Australians Gallery. It was a wonderful opportunity to connect with Elders including (now deceased) Uncle Ephraim Bani, Father Dave Passi and Aunty Flo Kennedy (my grandmother's first cousin).

Sitting with Uncle Ephraim one day, I asked him why there weren't many Islander young people involved in the cultural industry. He told me perhaps young people back home were too busy doing other things or getting caught up in bad company. At that moment, I gave him my commitment that I would change that. I did not know then how quickly this promise would become a reality.

As part of the inaugural exhibition, we included a miniature version of a traditional Torres Strait outrigger canoe. Prior to the museum's opening, as is cultural protocol, we held a blessing in the gallery space and named the canoe. Working with the Saibai community, mainly Mariana Babia and Cedric Waia, *Kulba Saibai* was born. It was magical. The museum director at the time, Dawn Casey, the first – and so far only – Aboriginal director, officiated the proceedings. It was special.

I worked at the museum for another year, delivering the *Paipa* (meaning 'windward') exhibition. It was a beautiful exhibition which showcased the migration of Torres Strait Islanders to Kuri Bay in Western Australia and to Townsville and Mackay in Queensland. During the development of *Paipa*, I met my grandmother's other first cousin, Grandad Seaman Dan (deceased) – one of our most treasured musicians, storytellers and performers. This experience solidified a strong cultural base and started to stir my desire to return to the Torres Strait.

## The first Torres Strait gig

In 2002, the Torres Strait Regional Authority – the peak Commonwealth agency for Indigenous affairs in the region – sought my services to establish the first Torres Strait Cultural Centre and to manage their regional arts program. At the time, my dad, my sister and her two children (Atima and Sione) all lived with me. We were a tight unit. I announced to Dad that we were going home to the Torres Strait. Dad resisted, noting that access to health services and education would be challenging for the children.

I did not want to upset Dad, so I decided it might not be a good move. Then I had a phone call from an artist at Kubin who changed my mind and ultimately my destiny. That was Billy Missi (deceased). He told me, 'We need you to help us.' So, Dad and I agreed I would go first. As always, I was the adventurer – perhaps a trait of first-daughter syndrome. Armed with one suitcase and an album of photos of the children, I was bound for the Torres Strait.

Three months in, I was missing my immediate family too much. Actually, I was missing Dad's cooking. I rang him twice every day, complaining that I was losing weight and only eating Weet-Bix. In my first few weeks on Thursday Island, Corinne Billy looked out for me. She would often come by with smoked snapper or a container of turtle (my favourite traditional food). I will be forever grateful for her generosity and kindness. Eventually, Dad relocated to Thursday Island after my pestering. Then came my sister, her children and my brother Shayne. During this time, Dad built a house for his parents on Hammond Island with help from his cousin Aunty Rosie and her husband Uncle Motulou Nai (from Tuvalu). It was a huge moment of change. Dad had been gone from the Strait for forty years and he was finally home. Life was blissful, and I enjoyed a successful career ... but then I got itchy feet.

In 2007, I was approached by the Department of Foreign Affairs and Trade (DFAT) to work in their Aboriginal and Torres Strait Islander Program. At the time, I was in the final stages of completing a Masters in Cultural Heritage, and it would take more than a job offer to lure me back to the 'cold country'!

## Canberra connection – take two

I returned to Canberra on the proviso that an esky of seafood would be sent down each month. This was very important, because sharing food is an essential part of our culture. Meeting other Torres Strait Islanders in Canberra was a huge blessing. We would often have cook-ups to share meals and stories about home. Young women – especially Kassmena Birch (now Chong) and Rachel Small (now Wawra) kept my world alive with their escapades.

During 2009, my world turned upside down. Dad got sick and passed away. I had been very close to my dad; everything started spinning. After his funeral, a huge emptiness remained. I visited Aunty Flo to work out why I continuously had itchy feet and struggled to settle down (still do!). She looked at me and said, 'You not only belong to us in the Torres Strait; you belong to the world.' That was hard to take in, but it made sense. I would forever be reminded of her kind words. She was a powerhouse. She had been instrumental in advising the plaintiffs in the *Mabo* case and I respected her greatly.

With that in mind, I remained at DFAT and carved out a very successful career in international affairs, including overseas assignments to China, Solomon Islands and Papua New Guinea.

## Torres Strait – take two

It would take nine years for my return to the Torres Strait. After working in Shanghai at the World Expo, Solomon Islands for RAMSI (Regional Assistance Mission to Solomon Islands) and Papua New Guinea on policy work, I relocated home directly from Papua New Guinea to head up DFAT's Torres Strait Treaty Liaison Office – a two-person office with fellow Islander Ugarie Mene. This would be the first time a Torres Strait Islander was in the role. It was significant. Managing the Torres Strait Treaty was one of my greatest achievements.

Working with traditional inhabitants, communities and government agencies on both sides of the border was rewarding and challenging. We were – and continue to be – the front line for Australia. It is a very serious responsibility. The Australian

Traditional Inhabitant Treaty Chairperson, Getano Lui, then team leader Willie Wigness from the Australian Federal Police and Uncle Saul Binjuda, previously from Australian Border Force, were integral to the way we led implementation in the region on treaty movements and border management. Our people, our voices, our way of doing business. I loved it.

Working on the shared border, constantly going on patrols and conducting community programs, my communication style and inclusion of others would showcase the importance of cultural values and diplomacy in implementing the treaty. With the support of my boss at DFAT, Ben Milton, I was able to achieve the impossible. Ben continues to be my inspiration and mentor. He is one of the most decent human beings I have ever met, and has had a positive influence on my life. His mentorship has enabled me to share the knowledge with others and to help them in their career choices.

In 2019, I was awarded a Public Service Medal (PSM) for outstanding public service in promoting the inclusion of Indigenous heritage in Australia's cultural and foreign policies. This recognised my work on the treaty as well as my work in China at the Shanghai World Expo 2010. This was a very proud moment because – to my knowledge – it was the first time an Indigenous DFAT officer had been awarded a PSM. I just wished Dad could have been around – but Ben was with me for the ceremony, and that meant everything to me.

In 2020, a unique opportunity presented itself. The minister for Indigenous Australians at the time, Ken Wyatt, appointed me as the first substantive female Chief Executive Officer of the Torres Strait Regional Authority (TSRA). It was an absolutely amazing experience. Here I was with international experience and solid cultural values, about to take the reins of the

Commonwealth's leading agency on Indigenous affairs in the region! I thrived in the seat and led a strong team of 154 officers. I advocated for the TSRA to recognise NAIDOC, International Women's Day and Indigenous recruitment and career development for staff. It was a substantial contribution. Bringing together diplomacy, cultural values, public service professionalism and integrity, I was in my element. Due to Covid-19 and restricted travel throughout 2020 and 2021, my itchy feet started to resurface. I was notified by DFAT that I had an overseas assignment. Here I go again … one suitcase.

**Canberra connection – take three and then some!**

I returned to DFAT for a short while in early 2022 and was deployed to relieve officers in the Pacific. First destination was Tuvalu. The only thing I knew about Tuvalu was that my Uncle Motulou came from there. It would be one of the most amazing and enriching cultural and professional experiences I have ever had. Second destination was Niue with stops in New Zealand and Fiji. I returned to Tuvalu because I loved it so much and then had a short assignment in Kiribati. Travelling the Pacific has been the ultimate dream job in 2022 and an opportunity to share with others about the Torres Strait and Australia.

**Growing up Torres Strait Islander – what has it meant?**

From my early life until now, strong cultural values and identity have been key to growing up Torres Strait Islander. Meaningful relationships underscored with respect and listening to and learning from those willing to share their story, knowledge and time, especially Elders, remain important. Education and a thirst for adventure have played their part in being a successful explorer – the blood runs deep from the Straits – we are a nation of navigators and seafarers!

Success to me – as an Islander, as a woman, as an Indigenous leader – is the ability to have a positive impact on other people. Our worldview is deeply enshrined through a cultural lens. These foundations were formed from an early age and heavily influenced by my grandmother.

The Torres Strait is a constant presence in my life. Whether I'm in the Torres Strait, on mainland Australia or overseas, being Torres Strait Islander is not a nine-to-five job or a tap that can be turned on and off at will. It is the very core and essence of who I am. I am truly thankful to Granny and to my dad for teaching me the key lessons that shaped the person I have become. If only they could have lived to see how the seeds they sowed back then have grown and touched so many in the world today.

The Torres Strait is forever in my heart.

# Do Your Best, Never Give Up

### Tetei Bakic-Tapim

My name is Tetei Bakic-Tapim. I want to tell you a story about mainland Torres Strait Islanders that was told to me by my grandparents, Francis and Agnes Tapim (née Ross), as they saw and experienced it. This yarn is important to me because it not only influences the opportunities and services I have access to today but also influenced how I grew up as a Torres Strait Islander person living on the mainland.

I was born in Cairns but moved to Sydney with my mum, Katica Bakic, when I was eight years old, for better educational opportunities. It was important to her that I spent as many school holidays as I could with my Townsville family, and so I visited my grandparents, my older sister Angelina Tapim, my older brother Francis Tapim Jnr and my extended family often.

My sister recently showed me a picture of her as a baby with our grandad, taken in the carpark of a place where all of us grandkids spent a lot of time, the Magani Malu Kes Information and Resource Centre in Townsville. Growing up, I always thought that my sister was the coolest person ever, because she got to live with my grandparents and whenever I visited she would show me what us younger ones would do at cultural family gatherings like funerals, tombstone unveilings, family reunions, et cetera. Together, we no longer stand for hours by the food to 'chase e fly' at these events, which I am grateful for.

My grandparents told me that the name of the Magani Malu Kes Information and Resource Centre was chosen to be representative of the Torres Strait Islander communities in the Townsville area. Magani Kes was the traditional name for the body of water in the Torres Strait, prior to it being renamed after the Spanish explorer Luís Vaz de Torres. Magani was a chief warrior in the Central Islands. Kes is an Eastern Island word for 'passage'. Malu is a Western Island word for 'boiling water', which refers to the turbulent sea before a storm or cyclone. The inaugural group of Elders who chose this name included the Tapim, Mabo, Akee, Day, Whaleboat, Kaddy, Noah, Wano, Getawan, Ebui, Cook, Ghee, Pilot, Martin, Doolah and Gabey families. Members of these families had a meeting in Townsville and decided on this name to represent the Eastern, Western and Central Islands.

Magani was established in 1996 after the Aboriginal and Torres Strait Islander Commission (ATSIC) first came in. At the time, you had to apply to ATSIC for funding. My grandparents tell me the story of how the idea of Magani started in a workshop in Townsville. The local Torres Strait Islander community identified that our people on the mainland were having difficulty accessing services set up for Aboriginal and Torres Strait Islander people. So, they rented an office at Atkinson House, in town on Stanley Street, opposite the police station. One office was for Aboriginal and Islander Housing (ABIS), and across the hallway was an office for Magani. They chose these offices to establish a base for operations, and so that ATSIC could see that Magani was a registered organisation. At that stage, Magani became an incorporated organisation, registered with the Australian Securities and Investments Commission (ASIC) and known as Townsville Magani Malu Kes Pty Ltd. The local community however, just referred to the centre as Magani, or Magani Malu Kes. My grandparents would say, 'Tell them – this is where we work. This is our base.'

A lot of people were involved in the submission to ATSIC. Magani didn't want to duplicate existing services – it wanted to be a resource hub to connect mainland Torres Strait Islanders to services already available to Aboriginal and Torres Strait Islander people. This is something my grandparents really made a point of when telling me about Magani. It was always about connecting our people to existing services. It was about recognition and representation, and about us having equal access to Aboriginal and Torres Strait Islander services. The Torres Strait Regional Authority (TSRA) received funding, but that was specifically for the Islands in the Torres Strait. Mainland Torres Strait Islanders only had access to services offered on the mainland. So, Magani wanted to improve access to housing, healthcare, supports for families and children (especially in court), education, and cultural programs to maintain language and dance on the mainland.

Community volunteers set up the office. They raised funds for office equipment such as stationery and a phone line. It was all hands on deck. Then Magani ran into some issues. Our old people didn't like coming to the building because they didn't like the lift – they were frightened of it because it was really old and rickety. So the organisation had to relocate. With initial funding from ATSIC, rooms were rented in Bluebell Arcade. Then funding was received from the Department of Employment and Training to purchase the building as a training and learning centre.

When I asked my grandparents about the leadership and governance structures of Magani, they explained that there was a board of directors who met monthly to discuss policies and strategic direction. The board members were all Torres Strait Islanders living in Townsville. At one point my grandad, Francis Tapim Snr, was the chief executive officer, and he oversaw the day-to-day administration as well as reporting to the board about operational matters. The board drafted a constitution for Magani, and there was a lot of consultation, led by Elders, about how to set up the organisation. There was a focus on culture and on economic development. My grandparents said:

> We wanted to make sure that even though we weren't living in the Islands anymore, we could maintain our connection to the Islands and practise our culture on the mainland – and we wanted to make sure that future generations wouldn't have to struggle like earlier generations had. We wanted to make sure that our communities were thriving, with stable housing, stable jobs, kids in school and access to health services appropriate to the needs of our old people and families. We had a lot of networks with various organisations, from working in sectors of government such as children services and corrective services, to name a few.

ATSIC had regional councils that were broken up into wards, and Townsville was its own ward that stretched west to Hughenden, south to Mackay, north to Tully and east to Palm Island.

Anyone within that region could contact Magani for information. At the time, there was also a National Conference for Torres Strait Islanders, hosted by the National Secretariat of Torres Strait Islander Organisations Ltd, where community members would come together to talk about their concerns and invite politicians to come and listen. The first National Conference was hosted by Grandad Steve Mam, who was the founder of IINA Torres Strait Islander Corporation, a Brisbane-based organisation. My grandparents acknowledge the work and example he set for raising awareness nationally to issues specific to Torres Strait Islanders living on the mainland. Grandad Steve Mam was a respected community member at the local, state, federal and national levels and a trailblazer of his time, and we saw him as a 'mamus'. In Meriam Mir language, 'mamus' means chief.

A criterion of the National Secretariat was that member organisations had to be legally registered bodies with a structured board and constitution. The member organisations from each state and territory would elect a representative to be part of the board of the National Secretariat. My granddad was the inaugural chair of the National Secretariat's board until it was abolished. The National Secretariat was deliberately set up this way so that Torres Strait Islanders living on the mainland were represented and could talk specifically about living on the mainland. The National Secretariat has not been replicated since the abolishment of ATSIC.

Something else I want to share from my grandad's time at Magani and the National Secretariat relates to the thirtieth anniversary of the Torres Strait Islander flag on 29 May 2022. Although the flag was designed in 1992, it was not officially recognised by the Australian government until 1995. There was a time, between 1992 and 1995, when it wasn't flown. It wasn't until 14 July 1995 that the governor-general of Australia, William Hayden, proclaimed both the Aboriginal flag and the Torres Strait Islander flag to be 'Flags of Australia'. My grandad tells me the story of how he went around the country, talking to all the state premiers and chief ministers of the territories about recognising the Torres Strait Islander flag and flying it alongside the Aboriginal flag on the mainland. The Torres Strait Islander flag was not automatically raised in every state at this point. He went with Grandad Benny Mills, who was the manager of the Office of Torres Strait Islander Affairs for ATSIC at the time, and together they spoke to the prime minister and ministers from 1996 onwards to gain their support. It was important to my grandad that Torres Strait Islanders be recognised as Indigenous people of Australia too.

Reflecting on some thoughts I have when I listen to my grandparents talk about Magani, I can't help but think that this was such a big project for everyone involved. I think about all the families involved and how their children and grandchildren have been affected because they were able to get the help they needed. I think of the old people who moved down from the Islands. English was their second or third language, and so talking to koleh people (white people) was not something they felt comfortable doing. My grandad talks about how our kids would end up in the courts with the very same language barrier, and I imagine how terrifying it would have been for their parents to receive a call from the police or from school or from some other koleh person, saying their kid was in trouble.

Magani held regular community meetings where we could come together to express our views in Creole, Meriam Mir and Kala Lagaw Ya. During the *Mabo* case, we were notified that state government officials intended to visit Townsville and talk to

Meriam families about their knowledge of the property boundaries back on Mer Island. The point of this visit was to confirm Grandad Eddie Koiki Mabo's land claim. Grandad Koiki often visited my great-grandparents socially, but on this weekend they all discussed land matters. My great-grandad rang my grandad and asked him to come over to be present for the conversation. This was important, because following that informal meeting my grandad had to translate for my great-grandparents from English to Creole or Meriam Mir, so that they could understand what the government officials were asking them. This has been in my thoughts a lot lately, especially leading up to the thirtieth anniversary of the *Mabo* decision, which was celebrated on 3 June 2022 in Townsville. Magani was influential in starting the first Mabo Day marches and NAIDOC events. When Grandad Koiki's grave was desecrated in 1995, Grandma Bonita Mabo decided to exhume his body and relocate his grave to Mer Island. Paul Keating was the prime minister at the time and endorsed this decision. Three Caribou planes were available to transport families from Townsville to Mer Island and back. My grandad (representing Magani), Grandad Benny Mills (representing the Office of Torres Strait Islander Affairs, ATSIC) and Uncle Edward Mabo (Grandad Koiki's eldest son) were coordinating this effort.

I located a transcript of my grandad speaking to the House of Representatives Standing Committee on Aboriginal and Torres Strait Islander Affairs in 1997, at a meeting dedicated to achieving 'greater autonomy for Torres Strait Islanders'. He spoke about Magani, explaining that 'what we have tried to do is start up some language programs which will identify [people] as Torres Strait Islanders ... starting with children,' including 'a pilot program that has been endorsed by the federal health minister ... to do with after-school care and vacation care programs'. The after-school care program, Kebi Kazil, included scheduled Torres Strait Islander language, dance and traditional craft activities and provided opportunities for kids to perform traditional dances at community events such as NAIDOC. The Department of Health and Ageing funded this program and later approached Magani to take over the running of Amaroo Early Childhood Centre, as they couldn't find anyone to run the centre's mainstream service. It would otherwise have closed down.

My grandad was advocating for the importance of maintaining our language and teaching young ones. I was moved reading this, because as a young person who continues to advocate and work for my people, it felt like a full-circle moment. I see a lot of my childhood in my grandad's statement, especially the part about demonstrating how I am a Torres Strait Islander. My grandad always told me that to be Torres Strait Islander is to demonstrate it. You do this by looking Torres Strait Islander (through dress and presentation), by speaking your language(s) and through cultural knowledge like dance and genealogy. For me, I do this by wearing my 'augemwali' (island dress) and a flower in my hair at cultural events, by listening to songs in Meriam Mir and asking my grandparents about our family back on Mer. My grandad taught me to introduce myself by saying 'I am Dowareb,' which is one of the eight tribes of Mer, and so 'I am a Meriam Le' (person from Mer). Reading the transcript of the 1997 meeting, I realised the significance of my grandparents' activism, both through the influence of Magani in my own life and its importance for the future of all Torres Strait Islanders on the mainland.

I grew up listening to a CD and DVD set called *Torres Strait Islander Railway Songs*. It came from the Aboriginal and Torres

Strait Islander Language Initiative Program, administered by Magani. This project was focused on maintaining Meriam Mir, the language of the Eastern Torres Strait Islands, through education. I loved listening to the old people sing in Meriam Mir at tombstone unveilings. It makes me so proud to know that Magani played a part in funding a project like this, so that these voices are recorded forever, and future generations can listen to them. That is something incredibly special to me and I keep his copy of the CD and DVD in my office at work. This small grant funding was given to ABIS to facilitate the recording and production of the CD and DVD. The singers included are Father Elemo Tapim, Grandad Victor Wailu, Grandad Potepa Captain, Great-Grandma Renah Tapim, Great-Grandma Merad Akee, Great-Grandma Anemah Ghee and Grandma Lilly Wailu. The dancers included are Grandad Robert Tapim, Uncle Aicey Day and Grandad Moses Gizar.

Magani lost funding after the abolition of ATSIC under the Howard government. Magani was a great example of mainland Torres Strait Islanders organising to have control over our futures, and that legacy remains today. I want the story of Magani to live on. I want us to remember how a small but proud community of Torres Strait Islanders living in Townsville envisioned a future where our people would have equal access to health, education and housing. Magani advocated to connect Elders and families to services that they wanted to be connected to, when maybe they didn't have the information or didn't know where to look, or didn't speak English or just wanted to talk to someone who looks like us, talks like us and understands our 'ailan kustoms'.

I want to finish with my grandad's mum's family motto: 'Do your best, never give up.'

Au essau.

# The Learning Time

## Ellie Gaffney

I had attended the Thursday Island State School for coloured children for approximately three years before my education, such as it was at this substandard school, was interrupted by World War II. We were evacuated to safer environments, and we lived down south, mainly in Brisbane for several years.

I never went back to school in my early years, and for the first few years down south, I was utilised by my parents and relatives as their guide in the big city and as their interpreter. At the age of twelve, I decided to put my age up to sixteen because I was big enough to pass for a sixteen year old. I then secured a job in a Brisbane cafe as a pantry maid, working from 6.30 am until 8.30 pm for three pounds, five shillings which in today's language is about $6.50. This brought into our household an extra and much needed income.

When the war ended and we returned to Thursday Island, I was fourteen years of age. I went to work as a shop assistant and receptionist for a pearling company, under the manager's supervision and training. The manager John Adrian taught me basic book work and office procedures, and enough typing (three fingers) to assist him. Later when the pearling company closed down because of the takeover of plastics, replacing the pearl shell in buttons and other things, I went to work at the local hospital as an assistant nurse. Whilst I was nursing, I found I absolutely enjoyed this type of work. It gave me great satisfaction to care for people and learn new things foreign to our lifestyle. During this period one of the nursing sisters I worked under, Dorothy Spencer, suggested to me that I should go down south to do my general training, because she said that I had the potential.

This suggestion motivated me to write away, making enquiries in regard to training as a nurse. Each hospital I wrote to acknowledged my enquiry and enclosed particulars, and the criteria required to be accepted as a trainee nurse. Unfortunately my scholastic standard was inadequate, therefore I set about to raise it. Now in those days, our caretaker in guidance for our wellbeing was considered to be our parish priest, so I set off to our local Anglican parish priest and poured my heart out to him. He suggested he would tutor me for fifteen shillings a fortnight.

I realised then I had to make an important decision, because I was only earning twenty-five shillings a fortnight. This would leave me only ten shillings to live on, which in today's terms is about one dollar a week. However, I decided to accept his offer and commenced the learning process, which consisted of attending his parish office two to three times a week, on an hourly basis. He would then give me prep one and two books to read, and he would take himself off to socialising with his white parishioners at bridge parties and other similar colonial activities of those days.

After a couple of months of this sort of set-up, I knew I wasn't getting anywhere, and into the bargain I had less money to spend. I received a letter from the Maitland Mater Hospital enquiring whether I had succeeded in raising my scholastic standard. I quickly approached our parish priest and showed him the letter. After he read it, he looked at me and the words that he mouthed to me were so crushingly cruel, I didn't wait around. With tears streaming down my cheeks I left, but I could still hear his words. I didn't want to believe them after all the time and precious money I had spent.

His words to me were, 'I couldn't raise your scholastic standard Ellie, I'm not a teacher.' I then asked him, 'Why did you mislead me?' He said, 'I wasn't misleading you, surely you didn't think for one minute that you would be able to do the nursing training and become a nursing sister. It is only for certain types of people.' I interpreted that to mean only educated white girls were able to do nursing.

Still crying, I went next door to the Roman Catholic church grounds where my basketball team were to meet and train on their court. I was early because of the circumstances. I started practising shooting goals and unconsciously I was taking my hurt out on the ball and basket by smashing my shots into the goal. This created an enormous racket whilst the nuns and the priests were preparing to pray at the 6.00 pm angelus.

The priest approached me to request that I quieten down, and to his amazement he found a crumpled and distraught athlete. When he enquired if I was alright, the flood gates opened and so did my broken heart. The priest at first was wondering what he had said to have made me cry so much, and so unashamedly openly. However he listened and said, 'Come with me, I would like you to meet a lady who may be able to help you.'

The woman he introduced me to was the Mother Superior of the convent – Sister Mary Florence. My story was related to this beautiful woman who said to me, 'I will assist you Ellie and you will become a sister.' With more tears, I enquired, 'Do I have to become a Catholic?' 'No' she said, 'only if you wish to.' 'How much will it cost me?' I asked. 'No money' she said, 'only hard work and dedication, and when you are trained, return and work with your people and encourage others to pursue advancement.' This advice was given to me in the early 1950s. This book is being written in 1988 and thirty years later we are still trying to work towards self-management in the Torres Strait.

The learning process with her took every spare moment we could find for the following twenty-six weeks to upgrade my standard from grade one to scholarship, which was classified as grade seven. I sat for her exams and passed with a mark of ninety-two per cent. During my learning time, Mother Florence had written to the Brisbane Mater Hospital enquiring if I could be accepted into their nursing school, should I pass my exams. The Mater was advised of my passing the exams, and they accepted me into their 1954 preliminary intake.

From here on it should have been straight sailing, but it wasn't. My parents and I scraped up all the money we were able to fly me from Thursday Island to Cairns, and then to go by rail from Cairns to Brisbane. When I arrived in Cairns, so did the monsoonal rains; all transport, particularly the trains, was held up for three weeks. When I eventually arrived in Brisbane I had an interview with the nursing superintendent, who was a nursing nun called Sister St Gabriel. She informed me that the prelim I was to commence with had already started, and there were two options left for me. I could return home and come back for the next prelim in six months' time, or find employment in

Brisbane until the next preliminary intake. A prelim is a group doing a preliminary nurse entry course prior to commencing nursing training.

I could have done neither for two good reasons. I had no money to return home, let alone return to Brisbane as well, and secondly I wasn't educated or trained for city work in those days. You see, I had become an Islander again. Once more the heavenly Father took care of me. Sister St Gabriel made a few phone calls, and advised me that she had secured a nurse's aide job for me at the Royal Brisbane Hospital for a few months. In that time I had to do a correspondence course through the Kelvin Grove Technical College to raise my scholastic standard and obtain a pass from the Queensland Education Department to be accepted by the Queensland Nurses Registration Board. I could then start my training at the Royal Brisbane Hospital until such time as I could transfer back to the Mater Hospital.

In the meantime I had to board out until I was accepted as a trainee. For those weeks my day would begin at 5.00 am. In the morning I had to walk a mile to the bus stop at Mt Gravatt, and that bus would take me to the Holland Park tram terminus, where the tram would take me to the Woolloongabba 'fiveways' bus stop to make the connection to the Royal Brisbane Hospital to start work at 7.00 am. I finished work at 4.00 pm, and the same transport cycle took place.

I would arrive home just after 6.30 in the evening, and each time my correspondence school papers were awaiting me to do and have in the post the next morning. It would be 11.00 pm by the time I had finished the papers, and cooked and eaten my dinner. Some mornings when the alarm rang, I would lie in bed and wonder tearfully why I was sacrificing myself when other girls were enjoying themselves in the warm weather on

Thursday Island. I believe it was my faith in the heavenly Father that kept me going.

I secured a pass of seventy-eight per cent when I did the correspondence course exam, and commenced my general training in April 1954 at the Royal Brisbane Hospital (RBH). When the time came for me to transfer to the Mater Hospital, I requested to be allowed to stay and continue my training at RBH. It wasn't because of lack of gratitude or disloyalty to Sister St Gabriel or the Mater, but it was because of the many friends I had made and grew to love at the RBH.

When I completed my general nursing training which I enjoyed immensely, I did my obstetric training at the Royal Brisbane Women's Hospital, and worked in Queensland and the Northern Territory.

My nursing life lasted for twenty-six years, which could have been longer if the Thursday Island Hospital Board had made a different decision in 1980.

Needless to emphasise the exercise was an expensive one, however I found the course very interesting and valuable. My reward is the education I obtained; it enables me to utilise and assert myself in almost anything and everything in my life and work.

This is an edited extract of
'The Learning Time' from *Somebody Now: The Autobiography of Ellie Gaffney, a Woman of Torres Strait*
by Ellie Gaffney,
published by Aboriginal Studies Press, 1989.

# Eded Mer (My Life)

## Thomas Lowah

### Some customs

Here are some of our traditions.

Before engagement, a young man would approach his uncles, especially from his mother's side. He would tell his uncle his intentions. The uncle would then approach the parents of the girl. If it was okay with them, plans would then be made as to when the nephew would be brought before her parents and relatives.

In the earlier days the wife's brother would be informed whenever one of her children were thinking of getting married. It would be the parents' duty to approach the uncle. His approval is sought. Sometimes he has to be forced to agree and consent. He then asks relatives and close friends for a meeting. At the meeting he would inform them all of the matter. There is rarely an argument on dislike after the uncle's consent to the matter.

The young man can then propose to their daughter before the two groups of families.

Three times he would ask the girl, 'Do you love me?' If she agrees she answers 'Yes' each time. The ring is then placed on the girl's finger, with some money placed beside it and some other presents.

Then, as in any marriage, the dates to announce the engagement and the wedding must be sorted out. As well as the dates, the invitations have to be organised and sent. The food will also need to be arranged, and here again the uncle will be the organiser, superviser, in short, the chief.

The relations would give whatever they could as a donation. The phrase used, 'We will help'. Now they might help with money donations but in the old days buying and selling was not known. Exchanging goods or barter was then quite common amongst the Islanders.

The uncle should again be the person responsible in matters such as this. The Ar-Wah-Deh, as in the Western Islands lingo, or Nu-Nei, pronounced nay, in the Eastern Islands lingo. It means the same as uncle. The mother's brothers would be more respected, noticed and understood. When an uncle on the father's side was being addressed by a nephew or a niece, they would call him Ba-ba; such as Thomas ba-ba, or David ba-ba. Whereas the uncle on mother's side would be ar-wah-deh.

In-laws are not supposed to call each other by name. Something would have to be given to cover the wrong you had made if you did. Much respect must be applied to any one of the in-laws, and we had to call them anything except their proper names. The word Towie, short for Towyan, and Nye-wet are Eastern Island Lingo which stands for in-law.

My cousin's sisters, to this day, address me as Bala T. Bala for brother and T for Thomas. I have a grandson named Thomas. My in-laws call him T-boy. One man was nicknamed Kusa, his proper name was John. Now, anyone who has an in-law by the name of John is called Kuso. If there is a Peter as an in-law the name Koza is used or Se-on.

Sometimes in-laws are not popular, and at times when mingling with them it causes embarrassment, awkwardness and difficulties. But one has to be respectful, polite and busy when they are around. The relatives, both of husbands and wives, are highly respected in the in-law relationships. They play a role in family life as well.

When a relative of the wife makes a visit the husband goes out to welcome the person or persons. The same applies the other way round. When in the house, either one will serve while the other talks. When presenting a gift to the in-laws, particularly the mother-in-law, it should be the best.

My mother-in-law smoked a clay pipe. Give her a new one and she would break the mouthpiece so that the bowl would be close to her cheek. I bought her a wooden pipe with a gold band and she just put it away as an ornament.

Once she asked me to make a spear for her. Generally you would ask someone for a bamboo spear if you did not have one yourself. But this was for my mother-in-law so it had to be special. I had to go 3 miles to get the makings.

After it was made with five prongs, securely tied and neat, it was presented to her. She kissed it and said, 'I will not use it.'

Years before I was born, students from various islands went to Mer Island (Murray Island) and later to Mabuiag (Jervis Island) to study. They were cared for by different families while there. The heart feelings between them grew, from friendship to a much stronger feeling. And so they thought of themselves as brothers and sisters and this has passed on to this day. Remarks such as 'You have a lot of cousins, aunts and uncles' are common. And no doubt, though not blood related, 70 per cent of these 'so called' relatives are better than the true ones.

One custom told to me by my own cousin is again of the older times. My cousin went spearfishing one day in a dinghy with his uncle. He was taught how to use the spear, the habits of different fish, how to recognise them in certain depths and where to aim. He finally speared a fish. His first. His uncle went with him to his home and told the boy's mother.

Crying, the mother said, 'Does it have to be?'

Her brother, the uncle replied, 'It is a must, otherwise we will be talked about.'

The part of the uncle then was to organise a feast at his own expense. This seems tough, but wait and read on. All the other uncles and aunts came along and just let the parents know what they wanted and took it. What they were not able to take away, such as coconut palms and other fruit trees and vegetable gardens nearby, they put up some sort of a sign, showing their ownership.

What was left was the house with sleeping things, the kitchen with cooking things and that was it!

This custom was banned because of it being too severe.

Another thing to know was never talk love or compliments to a girl or a woman when her male kinfolks are within hearing. A man could only joke with her mother, aunt or sister.

I could not reject the offer of going turtle hunting one night with an uncle and brother-in-law. We sailed to a reef about 3 or 4 miles away. Kai Maza or Big Reef. There were two other dinghies beside us. My in-laws, including the two with me, were some of the best in the Islands and respected for their skill.

So I was here, there and everywhere, trying to do most of the work. Everything prepared, I took over the job of rowing in the centre seat. It is customary that when the person at the bow goes over with the wap (spear), he must be replaced immediately by the person from the stern, so to hold the armu (rope).

That night was different. When Uncle speared the turtle, he then got back in the boat and called to me 'Tawie! Don't let it go for long, otherwise we will lose it.'

So I had to leave the oars to hold the armu at the bow. The turtle went straight for the edge of the reef. It was a dark night and a long stream of zagu (light) was made by the armu. When the turtle got to the edge it stopped and went straight downwards.

'It is a good one, Towie, do not lose it,' he repeated.

Well, I thought, this is it. I will either tell them I am not a fool or do it and make them think I have got guts. With just shorts on I let myself gently into the water, holding the armu. I followed, by diving, towards the turtle. It seemed a very long time before reaching it. The turtle did most of the work to the surface, all I did was turn it upwards.

They were ready up top and a sling was easily slipped around a flipper. When I got in the dinghy I stopped praying, the depth was roughly 5 fathoms. When we had the turtle in the dinghy and had rowed about 10 yards, a paddle was bitten by a shark. What size I do not know. I said another prayer.

I was highly praised next day. My mates came to see me and asked 'How was it?' They laughed their guts out. I had to laugh too.

To this day I have not been told why we younger ones were not allowed to eat the head of a fish, only the tail. Not the head part of a crayfish, but only the tail. Not to take the bottom end of a sugar cane but the top when sharing with someone older. I am sure this or those rules were more of a respect to anyone senior.

In short, what we were not supposed to eat was best in taste. The head of a fish and the lower part of a sugar cane were given to the elder ones for their benefit. Most children of the Islands believed that to eat the head of a fish or the lower part of a sugar cane would stop the child from growing. It was how the elders got the best of everything.

*

Preparations before a wedding consisted of donations of money, fruits and vegetables. Seafood will be provided by the boy's brothers, if any, and cousins and uncles.

On the wedding day, food is cooked by women in the kitchen and out in the open, in temporary fireplaces. Men butcher dugong, pigs, turtles, the parts to be baked underground, Kup Maori style.

The Islands provided the people with all their fruit, meat and vegetables and the sea provided the fish. The most popular method of cooking is called Kup Maori. This is food cooked underground.

Some years ago I was asked to organise an island feast at Ellis Beach in aid of the blood bank. One kind person tried to help and prepared a pit for the Kup Maori. I was asked to see it. It was not as I had expected. It was a pit 4 by 3 feet. So I told them to cover it up, otherwise somebody might have an accident. This is how it is done in the Islands.

The Kup Maori should be prepared by first raking or shovelling away dirt until the ground is slightly hollowed in a circle and to the size suitable for the amount of food that is to be cooked. Place dry wood, wattle is preferred because of the strong heat, around the edges, and place in the centre anything that would start a fire easily. Dry grass, timber chips, palm leaves and then build on with light timbers.

Quite a lot of wood is required and it must be built evenly around and upwards to the height of about 42 inches, about 3 feet and 6 inches. It is normally a square shape at the finish. Above the built-up timbers, empty three or four chaff or fertilizer bags of fairly big stones. Then light the fire at the bottom, a drop of kero can help. It will burn up the timbers and the stones will be warm to red hot when the timbers are all burnt. It is important to have no burning timber in the hole when the stones are spread out into the area. Place green sticks, light not heavy, from wattle (all must be green and have leaves still in place), on the stones before placing the food, usually wrapped up in banana leaves.

Immediately cover with green, light branches of leaves, coconut palms or banana leaves. Then bags, mats or canvas are spread over the whole works, so as to protect the food from dirt, which is then shovelled on, making sure no heat can escape.

For meat, such as pork cut into quarters, it takes about 2 to 2.5 hours to cook, while wrapped dampers, fish and vegetables take only 30-45 minutes. So they are always cooked apart from each other. One fire for the meat and one for the vegetables. So then you wait.

Kup Maoris are held at festivals, weddings, immediately after funerals, whenever there is dancing, singing or feasting with other island groups and for events we share together such as sports, fishing or hunting.

So back to the wedding ceremony where the older people would just sit or stand around joking. After the wedding ceremony, there would be feasting and dancing until the next day.

A few days later the married couple would make a visit to the bride's parents with money donated by the groom's relatives. This money we call mui-roog and the amount is supposed to be kept secret. The money would be put into the hands of the bride's mother.

A few nights later the couple would be advised by parents and uncles on what lies ahead of them and grant their wishes. The bride must not do any work until a little tea is made

She would be given a garden knife or a fishing line. Just something which signifies work, usually the knife.

Before money was introduced, vegetables and fruit were the main gifts. So far so good.

Now the bride must not call the groom's relatives by name. Likewise the groom. If the male addresses a female relative of the wife it would be 'woman'. If it was a male then it was 'Tow-iyan' or 'Towie' for short.

If a forbidden name is called and heard by the person or relatives, something then must be given to that person, and no more will be thought about it. Both parties are not known to expose themselves and be seen by each other, apart from the wife and husband of course.

It is a custom which the Islanders are careful about keeping, and is maintained by the elderly ones. A respect which is beyond some societies of people I know.

In the homes, when a few people are sitting and chatting, and when someone wants to pass between them, excluding children, he or she would bow from the waist while walking through. Not as though you were taking a walk through Lake Street.

Grace is always said before meals.

This is a joke I played once on my parents, aunts and uncle.

My father and uncle were both Kanakas. My mother and aunts could not understand enough English for them to understand what you will be about to read.

I was seventeen and my parents were proud of me, as being more educated. So I was asked to say grace.

This is how it was said.

'Holy, Holy Able. Fill your belly while you're able, what's left over stick 'em in your pockets.'

The response was a loud 'Amen.'

My cousin's brother nearly pissed himself laughing. I nearly choked trying to control myself. I did not have the courage to tell them. I couldn't now because all of them are dead.

## Dancing

The original dance of the Torres Strait Islanders was lifting each leg, with slow timing, about a foot off the earth. It was done, sometimes in single file and sometimes in twos and threes.

One of the dances was to imitate the dog trotting. The song would be 'Omai (dog) eser (like).' Dog-like, sung repeatedly.

One other was the movement taken from two sea gulls when one chased the other for a fish which the other one had. The movement is done as one.

Serarr-eser, gull-like. Like putting on a pair of trouser legs in quick succession or like using a sewing machine though much slower.

Mui-usiman was danced like stamping a fire out.

Dancing gear has different names, the head gear is dari. The necklace, dibi dib, was cut out from an arm shell. Two arm bands could be made out of lawyer cane or special vine, worn above the elbows and with enough room to put in a few bunches of crotons. Grass skirts and young, white coconut palms are tied around each ankle.

Drums are beaten by the non-dancers who sit in front singing. The whole is called Kab-g Kar.

Then there is the Tai-bo-bo dance introduced mainly by the men from Rotuma, Fiji and Sumatra. This was quickly taken up and put into more active and effective rhythm. Never was a love song danced.

War dances, and dances about boat sailing describing the four winds; Koky, the north-westerly; Sarger, the south-easterly; Ny-gai, the north-easterly and Zay, the south-westerly. Dances about the sea, reef breakers, diving, farewells and many others things, except love.

Dancing at weddings was always different. Invitations would be sent to the nearby islands, and to others if necessary. Dances would come in waves, children, young girls, married women, also the visitors.

The local married men, who called themselves Nigai, North East wind, some as old as sixty or seventy, would go in and dance a few times and with force. Then leave suddenly for home and no more was heard. Exactly like the north-east wind. It will blow for a little while then gradually dies away to a finish.

## Some games

There are many island love songs that are being danced in a European style. Each year, and an hour before the New Year, we would come together, at night, and walk the streets of the village, singing hymns to pass the old year out.

Right in the middle all would be quiet with a short prayer. A minute after the church bell, boos and tins and drums, whistling and shouting and singing.

The crowd would then move to one end of the village and go from house to house, singing and dancing. They would receive presentations and speeches from the owners, or someone on behalf of the same.

The speeches would be like, 'A happy new year to you all.' From the crowd, 'Same to you and the household.' Some encouraging words and advice on turning a new leaf.

The person would then present something, just fruit, vegetables or cooked food, and the crowd would shout, 'Eso' (thank you).

The men would dance and then move to another house. A special song is sung on this occasion, it goes:

Kole Iyawal-naglpa tin matamka mudia,

sagul au tonar ina-wer

Nu yau sagul au tonar – er.

Translated simply:

This is the time for fun,

let's hit the tins around these houses.

Time for fun, New Year's fun.

After all the homes had been visited it would be after sunrise and the collected gifts would be taken to a certain place for feasting.

As for sports, Edor, Tig, is the main game. Two parties, women versus men, and the rubbing play.

Two men would hold a woman and paint or paste her with flour. Three to four women would hold a fellow and do the same.

I remember my cousin and I chased a girl and she got into her house and locked it.

It was a grass house. A couple of bumps from us and the door went down. We got her painted. We fixed the door the next day.

Another sport was the fearsome Alag. These Alags are supposed to be devils who went about eating people. That is exactly what the person, or persons, would do when acting as Alags. One could guess what the people would do – run helter-skelter.

The Coming of the Light is another festival, to mark when the first missionaries landed on Darnley Island in the year 1870. Lately it has been celebrated as a festival in some cities in Queensland. Years before it was not much recognised, apart from the islands in the Torres Strait. Re-acting of the festival is held on the 1st of July annually.

Hiding and seek. This game is played in a small and in a much bigger way. For example when all the men of the village were together and working out elsewhere, the women would organise the cooking of food so secretly that not a male, or even children, were aware.

Arriving home the men would ask about why the tea was not cooked. Of course many excuses were made by the wives, such as, 'We are invited out tonight to Aunt Elsie's, so hurry and get cleaned up.'

The wife would leave while he was preparing. Soon after women's singing could be heard throughout.

'Ngalmun doob-de-emou-e', repeat. 'Gar-Kazil-ngalmun doob-de-emou-e.' Meaning: 'Find what we have hidden you men.'

The men would shake their heads. 'We should have known.'

Seeking for this hidden thing, sometimes the men would go in the wrong direction. Clues would be given by singing any other song indicating one of the four winds, but sometimes it would be a fake clue.

When it was found, the men would raise their voices shouting, 'Imanu', 'it is found'.

This time it would be a lovely supper cooked by the women. Fruits, sop-sop-pa-pye, which is yam, sweet potatoes and pumpkin, with chicken cooked in coconut milk and fish called sabi-sabi.

'What a lovely Doob,' the men would say.

A similar thing was done away from the village. Spears and wraps for turtle or dugong would be stowed away and a special place picked with gardens nearby, so vegetables and fruits were available.

When the fishermen brought in their catch and hunters their turtle or dugong, a Kup Maori would be made and fish grilled. Baskets were made from palm leaves to cart the food back to the village.

Since there was not any electricity, this game of hide-and-seek was played mainly at night when there was a moon.

In the summer, when it was too warm in the grass houses, it was a good time. At this time too the younger men who were not signed on the lugger boats and were still at home would get together to help people in the gardening or repairing homes.

A special rule we had was to give one day each week to help someone. This day was called 'Mission Day'.

The first to be helped were the elderly people who were not able. Secondly the widows, and lastly the people who try to help themselves.

The rule was laid down by the late Bishop of Carpentaria, Stephen Davis. Because St. Pauls Moa mission was governed by the Church, the bishop was the administrator for twenty-eight years.

The rule was gladly accepted by most, but disliked by a few who thought of some reasons not to continue with it. Being at that time the chief, I approached the bishop and mentioned the situation to him.

'I would like you people to carry out the rules of this special day for ever, if possible. It teaches unselfishness. It teaches you to love your neighbours, to give some time for others. So it stays.'

That was the sort of time when Doob au-Sagul could easily be arranged. The men one way, the women the other. Men and women seldom worked together.

Women would have the job of cutting grass for houses, or planting after the men ploughed. Boiling the billy and plaiting palm leaves for houses. Sometimes they were sent home when no special work was available.

We had also days for the church. A week to build the church and a week for ourselves. Of course this was agreed to by both the people and Superintendent Father Schomberg.

Church dues were paid, ten shillings from each male, our fathers, and 2 pound from each person out on boats, annually.

Every able body had something to do. The men would board a boat and go to a special place, where pebbles were filled in bags and brought back.

Women would sit around, each with a hammer, and break the bigger pebbles into size. The children would have the afternoon off to carry sand from the beach, about a hundred yards away.

A mixture of stones, cement, sand and water was turned over by two shovels, then packed into four pieces of metal which would form two blocks of concrete a time. We had more than a dozen of these set.

This went on year after year. The church, or the building, is not yet finished, but it is being used and consecrated. There a just a few things to be done before completion.

At my age then, I did not realise the importance of the work. If only I could express my feelings here and use the right word for it. I will be thankful to credit those responsible.

I think we were the happiest people in the world. With no money, yet we worked hard for ourselves and others and shared things amongst ourselves. These works were being done in every inhabited island of the Torres Strait.

This is an extract of *Eded Mer (My Life)*
by Thomas Lowah,
published by The Rams Skull Press, 1988.

# *Ina's Story: The Memoir of a Torres Strait Islander Woman*

## Ina Titasey as told to Catherine Titasey

### Living by the sun

When I was a small girl, close to Mama, time didn't exist. Life was simple. We had no clocks or watches and I'd never heard of six o'clock or midday. Like the rest of my family, I looked to the sun as a guide for what I should be doing and where I should be. The sun up above in the blue sky was my big, giant, shining teller of the time.

There was no noise during the night except for the three calls of the rooster, the last one as the sun started to rise. If I rolled over in the half-dark and heard the mut, small sunbirds, chattering to each other as they ate the seeds of the coconut trees, I knew it was time to think about getting up.

The day started just as the sun woke up itself, when the sky in the east turned pale, a light pink in the dry season and a light grey-blue in the wet. Cessa was living with Aka Neru, so Alfie and me slept in the same room in our island house, on the sand beach floor. Sammy and Lala were small then, and Rita and Benny weren't even born. Every morning we got up in the half dark, folded our calico sheets, rolled up our coconut mats with the pillows we been made from kapok seeds and left them in the room on the floor, ready for night-time. We only ever went into the rooms to sleep. Daytime was for outside in the sea, on the rocks or in the garden or in the cool shade of a tree with Mama.

Our cousin Sissy Alice helped with the chores. She stayed with her grandmother, Aka Wagab, who was Aka Neru's older sister. Sissy Alice came morning time and then did all the cooking and washing up, and I helped her when I wasn't playing or out hunting with Cessa and my brothers and cousins.

We always had a big breakfast which meant we could last till the main meal, supper, that we had in the afternoon. Breakfast was tea with damper or sabi sabi dhomboi, coconut milk dhomboi, made the day before, so we didn't have to make it in the morning. Sabi sabi dhomboi was lumps of dough cooked in boiling water till they floated. The dhomboi was then dropped in coconut milk and simmered in the saucepan over the fire in the kitchen. It was ready to eat when it had soaked up the rich coconut milk. If there was any leftover roasted or curried fish from supper the day before, we ate that also, sometimes with a cup of black Bushells tea, if we got some left from cargo boat time. If there was no leftover supper, we had to make damper or dhomboi in the morning.

Sometimes, if it was gath, low tide, us kids couldn't help ourselves and one of us grabbed a knife and walked out on the reef. The others followed. We always returned with something tasty for breakfast like clam or octopus or small fish we be spear. On the fire it went.

This kind time, we grew and hunted almost all of our food. Occasionally we got some supplies on the cargo boat from TI. Dad wrote out the next order and handed it to the skipper of the boat when they dropped off the supplies. The stores from the cargo boat were first taken to a storeroom at Aka Neru's house and later to the store Dad built for the DNA (Department of Native Affairs). Dad managed that store. There was fabric for sew that came on the cargo boat. Aunty Camilla, Dad's youngest sister, the thin one, did lots of sewing on a hand machine and turned out island dresses, lava lava, sarong, and bedsheets. She taught herself to sew and I used to watch her and admire the way she could make a dress out of a piece of cloth just by cutting in the right places and then sewing.

The cargo boat also brought big bags of rice and plain white Defiance flour and Bushells tea in blue-and-white paper packets, dhemkain things. Sugar also came in pound or two-pound paper packets and there were tins of lard for frying, IXL jam and Clive of India curry powder which I loved. Curry was made by frying onions, which also came on the cargo boat, in lard and curry powder. When it was nice and burnt, fish or shell meat was added along with coconut milk. Matha nice, yum!

Cargo boat time was exciting. It meant we had damper that I helped Sissy Alice make with the flour and lots of sweet sugar, like grains of sand, for our black tea. We never knew exactly when the cargo boat was coming. It arrived when it arrived. The great big-sail boat appeared and anchored off the edge of the reef, and a wooden dinghy rowed in with the supplies. If it was koey urr, high tide, good, because the dinghy would get right in up the beach and we didn't have to carry the cargo too far. But if it was low tide, yagar, we had to walk right out, the dead coral crunching under our bare feet, around the rocks and bombies and carry all the stuff in. It was hard work. When we were young, we carried the cargo because Dad told us to. When we older, we'd earn a few shillings from the DNA because it was sold at their store and so the profit went to the DNA.

Between cargo boats, after supplies had run out, we made damper and dhomboi from maniyotha, cassava. Gussi was a root that grew under a small bush and looked like a bunch of celery. It was pounded and then soaked in water before being made into dough for pakalolo, with root vegetables and coconut milk.

From as early as I can remember, I helped with fishing along with Alfie, Wrench and my cousins. Mama stayed home most of the time with the babies, as did the other mothers, but the boys went spearing and the girls fished off the rocks. If the men were home from diving kabar between neaps, they went spearing with sea glasses, a type of diving mask. The men used a long bamboo one-iron spear as they swam in the deep water off the reef. Papa Mothe, one of Grandad's illegitimate children, was the best spear fisherman. He'd always come home with a singay of fish, a lot of fish on a string of bush rope or a vine, whatever he could find. Usually he'd use the pula vine, a creeper with purple flowers that grows on the beach.

If the tide was out we couldn't fish, so we walked on the reef looking for anything we could eat. The reef was made of dried coral and had formed like a wall between the deep sea and the beach. It ran from one end of the island, Dogoman, to the other. When the tide went out, the coral wall kept the solwata, seawater, inside the reef like a lagoon, gungad, so we could still find fish. As the tide came in, it trickled through the low part of the wall till it slowly filled up the lagoon. Even when the tide was out, there was enough water in the lagoon for us to hunt under rocks and small bombies. The girls used a shorter spear than the men to poke under rocks. If it was my turn to use the spear, I ran the one-iron under rocks and coral, feeling the metal scrape over the hard surface, crunch, crunch. As soon as I felt the soft feeling that meant something alive, I gave a big poke and pulled out a small fish or sugu, octopus.

We looked for mudu shells and selpis, clam. We loved finding sugu and crab, bailer shells and ithay, which were spider shells that we boiled so we could pick out the meat. The cooked meat would be cut up for a curry, if we had Clive of India, and cooked in coconut milk. Otherwise we just sliced up the shell meat and ate it with our root vegetables or dhomboi or rice, if we had it.

Clam shells were tricky. There were different types: ones that grew from holes in rocks and coral and ones that grew on their own and could be picked up. This kind type were dangerous if your foot or finger got near to it as they closed hard and fast, the wavy edges as sharp as the cut-throat razor Dad used for shave with. If our toes slipped into the clam and it closed, the sharp edge could slice right through skin and bone. When I found a clam, I forced the knife between the closed edges and cut right down the middle where the muscle goes from one side of the shell to the other. Once that had been cut, the clam couldn't shut. Then it was easy to cut the muscle from the sides of the shell and scoop it out with my fingers to cook it. It was always important to turn the shell upside down so no one could come along later and cut their foot. Aka Neru and Mama taught me that.

Gardening was very important. Each family had a garden a long way from the village, on the side of the hill where the soil was good.

If a new garden had to be made, it was done at the end of the year, before the wet season started in December or January. We cut down the trees and chopped them into smaller pieces for make fire. We had to make a good firebreak around so the fire didn't take off. The ashes made the ground rich for the new garden. We knew when the first rain was on its way from the build up of fluffy cloud in the north-west. As soon as the first rain fell, the root vegetables like maniyotha, kumala, taro and yam went in the ground so they grew fat when the rain fell.

There was watermelon, corn, sugar cane and one special tomato tree that came from Grandad's time. The seeds from that tomato grew all the other tomatoes. The tomato was a big one and they grew in bunches. I'll never forget the smell blong, belonging to, that tomato: so strong and sharp like perfume. Even half-ripe, the tomato tasted good.

During mango season, we ate lots of mangoes. There was one mango tree in the village, but the rest of them were further away, at the mango saw, orchard. When they came ripe at the end of the year, before the rain started, us kids would take a woven basket and go and collect them from the branches that were so heavy with fruit they were almost touching the ground. Many mangoes would fall safely onto the soft blanket of leaves that collected under the trees and we picked these up also. Most of the mangoes were those sweet but stringy ones called 'government mangoes', probably because the government gave them out. There was one branch on one of the government mango trees that Grandad must have grafted on. That branch gave the best mangoes that were sweet and fat and soft and not stringy at all. We called them apple mangoes.

There was another fruit tree that Grandad had grown that ripened at the same time as the mango. It was called the jam tree, not like a mango with one big trunk but more like a mulberry tree with thinner trunks. It had a berry that started out green and turned black when it was ripe. It was like a blueberry. No one knew how to make jam like in the IXL tins so we just ate the berry straight from the tree.

When wongai fruit, like small fig, was in season in about September, we would take out the seed and soak the flesh in water to make it soft. While it was soaking, we made dhomboi and boiled it, stirring so it did not stick to the saucepan. Once it was cooked, and the coconut milk was simmering, the dhomboi and the wongai were added to it so it was like sop sop, root vegetables cooked in coconut milk, but nice and sweet.

Coconut milk was a big part of our diet and we made it nearly every day when we cooked fish, damper or sabi sabi dhomboi. After the coconut was skinned and the water emptied to drink later, the shell was split using a knife. The meat was scraped out using the metal scraper, madhu, attached to a wooden stool that Dad had made. Our madhu was one half of a door hinge that Dad had got off some old doors from Grandad's place. Dad was clever like that; he knew how to make do. The half hinge was nailed onto the stool and then Dad filed the end to make teeth, like a comb, that scraped the coconut flesh. The scrapings fell into a big enamel dish and were then soaked in a cup or two of water for a while. At first we used to squeeze the milk out by hand, but then we started using the netting husk from the coconut tree, called yoeway, which opens out like a mat. A handful or two of the coconut scrapings went into the yoeway and we squeezed the milk out into another enamel basin. More milk could be squeezed out with the yoeway than with just our hands.

Whenever us kids got hungry during the day, one of us climbed a coconut tree and cut down nuts because we always carried a knife. We took green coconuts because they were easier to skin with our teeth. One coconut gave us water to drink and meat to keep us full until supper. After sticking the knife into the three soft black holes on the top and drinking the water, we cracked open the shell and dug out the crunchy white meat.

There were also meke nuts, sea almond nuts, as well as bananas and pawpaws that got us through to the afternoon.

We didn't only eat coconut. We relied a lot on coconuts fronds for making mats and boey for our houses. Boey were the coconut fronds, split down the backbone and woven to make a section of plaited coconut matting to become the roof, walls and windows of our island houses. Baskets were made from fronds which were split down the middle with a knife. The hard stem became the lip of the basket and we wove the bottom. The baskets were used for almost everything: storing our clothes because we didn't have wardrobes, collecting fruit and vegetables from the garden, carrying the sand for our sand beach floors and for fishing. The women and girls did all the weaving and it was a great time for small yarn and big laugh, for sing and dance, bambai, later if we got time.

Even though they got time for dance, the women kept an eye on the sun. They cooked the dinner, and the men, if they were home, looked for firewood. The wood was kept in the outside kitchen of the island houses on big logs up off the ground so that it could never get damp.

If us kids were out fishing or playing long way from home, we looked out for the sun. As soon as it was in the middle of the sky, it was time to clean the fish or gut the sugu out on the rocks and head home. Everyone knew to be home by the time the sun was in the west to get ready for supper. The big meal was usually fish, three fish for our family, fried, roasted or made into soup, zura.

We could only fry fish if we had lard from the cargo boat. Mostly it was zura fish and roast fish, roasted over a ground fire with stones to hold some irons across the fire. These irons took the saucepans for boiling coconut milk or making curry. The ground fire was in the kitchen of our old house, in a section that jutted out so the smoke could go out a hole. We had to have supper cooked and eaten and have washed up before the sun went down. If we were late having dinner, which wasn't often, Dad lit the hurricane lamp so we could wash up.

After supper, when everything was cleaned up and the sun had gone down, we went outside. On moonlit nights, Dad and Mama would sit on the beach with the other adults and kids from all the different houses and we played till bed time. I remember one game, Alligator, though I am pretty sure we didn't know what an alligator was. We all lined up holding onto each other's waists. One person, the alligator, is on the ground crawling and trying to grab at people in the line, to make them 'in' so they become the alligator. As each person moves to get out of the way, the alligator then goes for someone else in the line. We loved that game and kids of all ages would play.

We learned songs and island dancing from the aunties and uncles who knew the steps. Dad was a good island dancer and he loved singing the island songs too. There would be someone with a big wooden warup, drum, and someone with the thrum, a kerosene drum turned upside down. We used branches as drum sticks on the thrum. I learned to love music, to need to sing and to make music.

Every month all the families cleaned up the fallen meke, sea almond, and mango leaves and the fallen whole coconut fronds, boey kuik, in the village. They were all piled onto each other on the beach and lit up to make a big bonfire. I loved bonfire nights.

Then, it was time to go aus, unroll my coconut mat and lay down next to Mama while she stroked my head and I fell off to sleep. During the naygay, the doldrums, when it was steaming hot, we threw our mats near the beach under the stars and lego sleep, settled down for sleep, and Mama stroked my head while I listened to the splash of the water on the shore and the rustle of the coconut fronds that lulled me to sleep. I needed a good night's sleep so I could get up when the mut were singing in the coconut trees and the eastern sky came light grey or pink, before the sun came out and turned the sky blue.

## What I learned

When Cessa and I were little, we were taken away from our family. That was soon after a man visited Naghir. He was the reason we were sent away.

Dad told us to call this man Father. It didn't make sense. We already got one father, Dad. We didn't get to call this strange man Father much because we stayed away. He was strange looking, being white. I wasn't frightened of him which makes me think he wasn't the first markay, European, I seen. We called white people markay, meaning white devil, which is what Islanders thought the first white people were: spirits. He was strange, pale compared to us who were really dark. This Father man had straight hair, very thin, like blades of the aus grass that kept out the rain from the top of our houses. Except his hair hardly covered his shiny white head.

The second reason we stayed away from this white man was because Dad had taught us never listen to adult conversations. Not that I could have understood Father when he talked. He spoke a language I didn't know, English. We spoke

Broken English on Naghir and I could only make out a few words of Father's language here and there like 'lugger' and 'Thursday Island'.

Then again, maybe I wasn't scared of this white devil because Dad was there and Dad looked after us and always kept us safe. I trusted Dad. He'd never let us down. I no sabe nothing about time except dry season and wet season, time for plant garden, time for pick the maniyotha, cassava and kumala, sweet potato. There was canoe time in the naygay, doldrums, when the people from Daru come down for trade pandanus mats. Also there was neap-tide time, spring-tide time, time for get up in the morning, time to come home for kai kai, eat.

A long time later I learned that when Father visited that time it was the year of our Lord, one-thousand, nine-hundred and thirty-three. Cessa and me were five and a half.

Not long after Father left from that first visit, Dad told me and Cessa and our older brother, Alfie, we had to pack our clothes because we were going to the convent.

This is an extract of
*Ina's Story: The Memoir of a Torres Strait Islander Woman*
by Catherine Titasey, 2011.

# The Other
# Indigenous Australians

**Donisha Duff**

'The Torres Strait? Where's that?'
'Is that part of Australia?'
'Do you need a passport to get there?'

These are just a sample of questions I am asked when I identify as a Torres Strait Islander living in urban, contemporary Australia. While many Australians are aware that Aboriginal peoples are the First Nations people of Australia, they are not as familiar with the First Nations Australians of the Torres Strait.

I was born on Waiben (Thursday Island) and spent most of my childhood swimming and fishing in the waters of beautiful Zenadth Kes (Torres Strait). I am of both Aboriginal and Torres Strait Islander descent, but I spent my childhood in the Torres Strait and living a Torres Strait way of life.

Historically, Waiben was a trading hub for peoples from Indonesia, the Philippines, Papua New Guinea and Japan, and for Pasifika, Aboriginal people and Torres Strait Island-ers long before international borders were established. It was, and is, a multicultural community in which being different was embraced and celebrated. As a young child, I remember going to community gatherings and experiencing the differ-ent smells, foods, language, singing and dancing from other cultures.

When my family moved to the mainland of Australia, it was very evident that this experience was not the norm for 'main-stream' Australia. I was often the only Aboriginal and/or Torres Strait Islander child in my class at school. My family was often the only culturally distinct family in our school and commu-nity. There were very few ethnic or migrant families in regional Queensland.

Most often, the response from my teachers and other school kids when I identified as a Torres Strait Islander was, 'Are you sure? You don't look Aboriginal.' Clearly, I wasn't the stereo-typical dark-skinned version they were used to seeing in storybooks. More recently, I am often mistaken for being of Māori heritage. On my first visit to New Zealand as a young woman in 2004, local Māori people even asked if I was sure I wasn't Māori, as I 'looked like one'.

Being a Torres Strait Islander in Australia today, I am con-stantly educating people about who I am, where I am from and how we are different from Aboriginal Australians.

## Breaking stereotypes: the 'first' in many areas

Growing up as a young girl on Waiben, it was difficult to envi-sion what my future could be. At that time, there weren't any First Nations doctors, lawyers or other senior professionals to look up to and follow. The majority of professional or senior positions were held by non-Indigenous (white) people. Despite these challenges, it became increasingly clear to me that attaining and completing an education would broaden my future options. My parents moved my sisters and I to mainland Australia so that we would have more options in our future.

When I followed the path of my sister to study at Griffith University in south-east Queensland, we were the first generation of my extended family to attend university and complete undergraduate degrees. University was a completely different experience, as there were often only a handful of Aboriginal and Torres Strait Islander students. Griffith University, like many other universities, established a space dedicated to supporting Aboriginal and Torres Strait Islander students. The Gumurrii Centre was a safe space to seek academic support and social interaction.

In 2013, I became the first in my family to graduate with a postgraduate university qualification. Indeed, I was also the first Aboriginal and Torres Strait Islander to graduate with a Master of Business Administration (MBA) from the Australian National University in Canberra. The Tjabal Centre played a significant role in providing academic and social support.

## Giving back – it's our way

Despite having few role models and mentors along the way, I am passionate about creating greater opportunities not just for myself but for other Aboriginal and Torres Strait Islanders.

After graduating with my MBA, I joined the board of the start-up not-for-profit Stars Foundation, which aims to assist young Aboriginal and Torres Strait Islander girls and young women to graduate high school. I was struck by the familiar stories of being 'first in the family' from girls who needed peer support to stay in school. They had big dreams, but they faced a number of unique challenges that made it difficult for them to succeed. Our programs assist these young women not just academically but also by giving them time and space to discover what they want to do in the future. Thanks to the tireless work of our Stars teams, we are achieving an average of 97 per cent Year 12 graduation and 93 per cent successful transition to work or further study or training. I am immensely proud of what we are able to achieve in supporting our young women to complete school and pursue their dreams. This is a change that will have generational impacts in years to come.

**Occupy space**

As the other First Nations Australians, we have a unique identity and experience that should be celebrated. However, there is a demonstrated lack of knowledge about Torres Strait Islanders (and Aboriginal people) and the challenges we continue to face. At a national political level, this is translated into the development of substandard policies and legislation, which negatively affects our families and communities and locks us in a cycle of poverty and disadvantage.

In 2022, I was preselected as the Labor candidate for the federal electorate of Bowman, south-east of Brisbane. I was one of only two Aboriginal and Torres Strait Islander Labor candidates in Queensland in the 2022 federal election. While I was not elected, it provided a platform to raise awareness of the need for greater representation, economic development and better support services for Aboriginal and Torres Strait Islanders, and hopefully encouraged other First Nations Australians to consider politics as a vehicle for change.

As 'first in the family' Torres Strait Islanders, we must take opportunities to raise awareness and seek to change the circumstances of our families and communities. We must break the negative stereotypes of our people and step into spaces that are not traditionally ours. We must remain resilient and unapologetic in making room for future generations to follow us, so that we can plant the seeds for generational changes.

As firsts, we will pave the way for many more firsts to come: first-generation professionals, first-generation leaders, first-generation entrepreneurs and even the first-generation prime minister.

# A Torres Strait Islander Mainland Story

## John Doolah

My story of growing up Torres Strait Islander in Australia is actually four separate stories combined into one. The four main voices are those of an Ailan man, a Christian, an Australian and an educator. For the purpose of this document, I feel there is no need to explain my Christian, Australian and educator identities – but my Ailan cultural identity, yes, I feel I need to elaborate. I am of Eastern Torres Strait heritage, Meriam Le and Erubam Le. I will begin with my take on the historical situation of my people and an account of our Ailan and South (mainland Australia) stories.

The history of Ailan pipel in the Torres Strait post-contact and our migration down south to mainland Australia is well documented. Today a small percentage of Ailan pipel live in the Torres Strait homeland, with a large Ailan population settled on mainland Australia. The typical Ailan story begins with our fathers, mothers, uncles, aunties and grandparents moving out of the Torres Strait, escaping the restrictive mission life and the racist colonial government policies and looking for jobs.

Not all migrations are the same. Families migrated for different reasons and in different circumstances. For Ailan pipel of my generation, our parents and grandparents were from the early post-contact generations. They were labourers with limited mission education. They worked hard, struggled, fought hard and provided for their families. They were, and continue to be, our role models. Even if we break the moulds with our achievements, do things they were not given the opportunity and freedom to do, we have built and continue to build from nothing. The nothing is not about what we do not have but about what was and is taken away from us, what was denied to them and us. This is the foundation of the struggle we continue to build on. It is our resistance, our experience, and it is not just the struggle of the individual: for we as a people, it is the Ailan story!

## Who am I?

Most Ailan pipel know me as Cyril. I was born on Thursday Island (TI) in the 1950s. My mother Harriet Doolah (née Bourne) and I moved from Mer in the early 1960s to live on Erub with my dad, Gara Doolah, in the Doolah family home at Esem. The move to Erub was at the request of Dad's uncle, Dato (Grandfather) Charlie Doolah. I have childhood memories of my early years in Zeub Village on Mer. I remember my Grandfather Sina Jib taking me to his garden in Mer, where he would cut his Daru tobacco into tiny pieces and use the golab (dried banana leaf) to roll the tobacco and smoke it. I remember spending time at the home of my mother's sister, Darling Mama, the wife of Uncle George Mye. Their son Abu and I played together, and I remember the first time I tasted Kraft cheese was while staying at their home in Mer.

When we lived in Esem Village, the house was very high, with no front steps and no front door but a long back staircase. I remember eating soft butter from a tin with a nice picture of a cow on it. I remember going to preschool in Erub, where we drank powdered milk.

## Childhood on Thursday Island

After Dato Charlie Doolah's passing, we (the Doolah family) moved with Nene Charlotte Doolah (née Reuben) from Erub to live on TI.

I have fond memories of my childhood on TI, living with Nene Charlotte and five of my cousins. We were poor. I came to understand the meaning of this word 'poor' through my childhood experiences. I ate discarded apple cores that people dropped on the ground, and I washed and ate the discarded seeds of salty plums. I remember walking into the kitchen in the middle of the night hungry and looking for food in the empty kitchen cupboards. We did not have the luxury of owning a fridge.

But love was there, and we had that very strong family connection, and we shared. At night I would massage the cramps in Nene Charlotte's arms, body and legs. One time I massaged Nene's cramps until early morning, when I saw the sunlight coming through the louvres on the windows of our rented flat.

On TI we lived on the main road, Hastings Street, almost at the intersection of Hastings and Summers, where the Thursday Island Primary School was located back then. I later became aware that the year I first went to school was the year the native school and the white school combined. Prior to that there were two separate schools on TI, one for the natives and the other for the white kids. I am not 100 per cent certain whether the half-caste kids were at the native school or with the white kids at the white school.

Nene Charlotte took us to church every Sunday. At first we went to the All Saints Anglican Church on Erub. We continued by going to St Bartholomew's Anglican Church on TI. Then Nene changed to the Pentecostal Church, when Uncle Edgar Williams and Uncle Peter Tapau began to hold their church meetings in a tent near the IIB store. I remember being involved with the Sunday school activities at the Pentecostal Church. I was eleven when, in 1969, we travelled with Ansett Airlines down south to mainland Australia for the first time.

## Life down south

I have lived down south ever since. On the mainland, I lived with my parents. My grandmother returned to TI with my cousins. My parents joined a new church, the Universal World Church, which had begun in 1968, a year before we moved from TI. We lived in several towns and cities in Queensland. I lived with my parents in Mackay and sometimes with other relatives, in places such as Hughenden, Blue Water, Brisbane, Townsville and Innisfail, and then we moved to Rockhampton the year I left school.

After leaving school, my first job was on the railways with my dad, in a relay gang in Rockhampton. I later moved from Rockhampton to Brisbane to live with my Big Daddy (Eldest Father) Elia Doolah. In Brisbane I joined a railway construction gang, working for Wacol Construction. The Wacol

Construction gang was responsible for track and turnout construction throughout the Brisbane CBD, south Brisbane and the suburban lines towards Beenleigh. The new trackwork was for the electrification of the tracks ahead of the 1988 Brisbane Commonwealth Games.

The ganger (supervisor) was a Badu Ailan man called Iona Nona, and the leading hand was my brother Poy Pensio. When Iona moved back to Western Australia, Poy became the ganger. The gang members were predominantly Torres Strait Islanders from Western and Eastern Torres Strait. Two of the last major jobs we did involved connecting track across the Merivale Bridge and the Brisbane River for the first time. This trackwork connected the New South Wales track to Roma Street Railway Station in Brisbane, and the rail network of north Brisbane to south Brisbane.

In 1979, I left the Brisbane gang and moved to Sydney, where I worked for Caddies Construction, a private railway construction gang located at Homebush in Sydney's inner western suburbs. The trackwork we did was for the Homebush–Strathfield connection, near what is now Homebush Olympic Park. At that time, we were the highest-paid railway labourers in New South Wales. Later I moved to the NSW government's State Rail Authority and was a ganger and manager of track construction for more than fourteen years, supervising new trackwork, turnouts and crossovers throughout New South Wales. One project my gang worked on was the construction of track near the New South Wales and Queensland border, on a section of track called the 'border loop'. My gang of between twenty and thirty men was composed of Ailan men, Australians and men from non-English-speaking backgrounds.

# Education

During that time, my gang constructed crossovers for the Hunter Valley rail line, north of Sydney. One day we were working on a section of the track near the Warabrook Railway Station, opposite the University of Newcastle. I stood on the track, watching my men work, and looked over to the university. I started thinking about how I had worked half my life with my hands – next, why not work my brains in education? A few days later I applied for leave without pay and enrolled at the university. To my surprise, I was accepted to do a bridging course, but I was afraid and changed my mind and returned to work. Two years later, a new head of the State Rail Authority took over. The new management offered redundancies to workers. I saw it as an opportunity and the only way I could leave the railway to do serious university study.

Before I left the railways in the early 1990s, I was already involved in the church. My parents were still in the Universal World Church, the church I had grown up in. Now, I began balancing my studies with church activities, including attending the annual international conventions of the Universal World Church in Los Angeles. It affected my studies, and at times I would switch from full-time to part-time study to catch up. Two years after I enrolled at the university, I graduated with a Diploma in Aboriginal Studies. Then, in 2004, I completed a double degree, with a Bachelor of Consumer Science (Applied Science) and a Bachelor of Aboriginal Studies. After graduating, I enrolled in postgraduate studies and was offered contract lecturing in Aboriginal Studies at the Wollotuka School of Aboriginal Studies at the University of Newcastle. While lecturing, I neglected my postgraduate studies because I was still balancing my work with my church activities.

When my teaching contract ended, I enrolled in full-time postgraduate studies but continued sessional teaching. I completed a master's degree in Aboriginal Studies, enrolled in a PhD and graduated in 2021. Before I submitted my PhD thesis, I secured a lecturer's job at one of the leading universities in Australia. Almost a year into my new job, I am now typing this document as a lecturer in Indigenous Education. It is my blessing and a continuing story, building something from nothing. One thing I have learnt is the importance of continuous learning through one's own lens, knowing and acknowledging who and where the self is in a changing social world of relationships.

## Ailan culture

The word 'culture' has a very broad meaning. I understand it through my own lens: it is how I see the world, and how I choose to behave and navigate my way through social relationships. Now, for me, it is not only Ailan culture; it is my culture, it is who I am, from my childhood growing up Torres Strait Islander in Australian society!

When I returned to tertiary studies in the early 1990s, I found it very hard, because I thought I had to learn how to learn. I had finished high school before graduating Year 10. One important thing I learnt was that from the beginning of my university studies, I was dealing with that baggage of exclusion. Like many Indigenous children in Australia, then and now, during my early years of schooling I was excluded from education because of the colonial policies of assimilation that were still embedded in the Australian education system. I tried to understand the concepts of another culture, of a different worldview and what I understood to be the Western way of thinking. In the end I found I could not learn that way, using that approach.

I tested my theory by asking some of my non-Indigenous fellow students about some of the topics we were discussing in class. I found that their understanding was different to mine, but I understood other things, just as important, which they could not understand and did not see. This enriched my learning experience and allowed me to contribute more in class as a student. In a class of almost forty students, most had just completed Year 12. For one of our essay assignments in Consumer Science, I received a mark of forty out of forty, the highest mark in the class, in which I was the only Indigenous student.

In one of my Aboriginal Studies classes, where all the students were Indigenous, we changed our approach to group assignments because we found that most students in the group did not understand the question and only one or two were contributing to the discussion. So, we broke down the assignment question using our Indigenous understanding and found that after that we all contributed and received a good mark for our efforts.

My education journey was in understanding who I am, that there was no need for me to change to accommodate the Western way of learning and to remain who I am and learn through the combination of the Western way and the Ailan way. Later on in my teaching career, I came to understand this way of learning as two-way learning, in an education space where Ailan and koleh (Western) knowledge meet.

I believe this is what Uncle Koiki did when he formed the first Black community school in Townsville. It was about inclusivity in education, because we as Ailan pipel, with our Aboriginal brothers and sisters, have been left out of the Australian education system since colonisation. I heard from our old pipel that it was about getting the best of both worlds – that of the koleh and Ailan – and finding our own place in Australian society.

I know of many Ailan people who left the Torres Strait to settle on the mainland, some of whom have since returned to the Torres Strait to live. Not all Ailan pipel have relocated to the mainland. Some of our families never left. My generation is the generation whose parents were the first to move to the mainland to look for work in the 1960s and 1970s. My grandparents and parents knew the meaning of moving to the mainland. It is about moving to the land of Aboriginal people.

Growing up Torres Strait Islander in Australia means growing up on Aboriginal land. I doubt whether the younger Ailan generation who were born on the mainland are fully aware of what it means for Ailan pipel to resettle on Aboriginal land. I think that maybe what Uncle Koiki's friend remarked about him living away from our homeland is a good reminder for us Torres Strait Islanders growing up in Australia that we are still Ailan pipel. We are not disconnected from our homeland. The cliché is true: although Ailan people may be separated from the Torres Strait, the Torres Strait cannot be separated from the Ailan pipel.

# My Link to the Torres Strait

## Velma Gara

My parents decided to move away from the Torres Strait to pursue opportunities on the mainland. They decided that it would be best for the family to leave the saltwater country and travel to the unknown – new food, language and environment. I was too young to be involved in the conversation about the move. Did they go through the pros and cons, was it their faith, or did they think that because they were together, they could conquer the unknown?

I was born in 1963 and my sister, Patricia, was born in 1965. I'm still amazed that my parents took this journey from Thursday Island to the northwest Queensland township of Torrens Creek. Sadly, my parents are deceased, so I cannot ask them these questions. My father, Moira Gara, worked on the railways. There was a great push for labourers to work in western Queensland and to travel to the western part of Australia. My mother, Martha Gara, née Sailor, was a cleaner at the house where train drivers spent their rest times.

What I can remember of Torrens Creek was that it was hot and dry, with not many people but a lot of dust and flies. The school was one big classroom with students from grade seven down to grade one. There wasn't much to do in the town. I remember we would go to the creek to swim and Mum would make assis (ashes) damper. We'd have family visit from Hughenden, where they were staying while working on the railways too. I vaguely remember Dad's family visiting, and Mum's family from Bamaga, but not much else.

We were pretty isolated, and the only form of transport we used was the passenger train. We'd travel to Hughenden to spend Christmas with family, and I can remember being traumatised when we had to kill the pig and make pig-blood dish. Although we were away from our extended family, Dad did try to teach us Island language songs. We have recordings on the reel-to-reel recorder.

In hindsight, if Dad had lived longer, I would have been taught to speak Miriam Mir. But everything changed when he died in 1970. My mother decided to bury him in Townsville, and we moved there. Patricia and I went to Railway Estate State School, followed by Townsville State High School. We lived nearby, so it was hard to make up excuses not to go. The primary school was across the road from our house, and it took about ten minutes to walk to high school. The only time we didn't go was when it rained – no-one carried an umbrella or wore a raincoat to school; you either got soaking wet or you stayed home.

My mother continued to work as a cleaner at the railways and was looked after pretty well. She kept working until she had to stop for health reasons in the early 1980s, due to diabetes. She had one of her legs amputated and we had to change our eating habits to help her. English wasn't Mum's first language, so when doctors told her about her leg, my sister and I had to translate for her, as well as at dietitian's appointments, physiotherapy appointments, and back at the doctor's for her medication. We changed our lifestyle for her with no complaints.

Getting an education wasn't a priority; it was something that just had to be done. How I coped with school was by playing sports. In primary school, I loved netball and would spend countless afternoons practising my shooting. Once I got to high school, my practising paid off and I played representative netball for Townsville. However, by chance, a teacher who coached basketball asked me to fill in on a team and, as they say, the rest is history.

I was a late starter to playing basketball: at sixteen I filled in on an under-eighteens team, and three years later I made the Queensland under-twenties team to compete at a national championship in Sale, Victoria. Apart from travelling to Thursday Island for family gatherings, I had never left the Sunshine State before. At the nationals, we made the grand final and got beaten by Victoria. If there hadn't been girls I knew in the team, I don't know if I would have gone to Sale. Luckily, there were two other girls from my club team in Townsville, so it was an okay trip. I hardly made the court, but I was okay with that because I was still learning the game.

My identity as a Torres Strait Islander was never mentioned or questioned. In 1983, I received an invitation to attend the Australian Institute of Sport Basketball Program, now known as the Basketball Australia Centre of Excellence. I spent a week in Canberra, where I enjoyed the training and saw what elite athletes do to better their game. I was never asked about my family, where I was from or why I had an afro! Looking back, I don't think the other players were interested in my background. Maybe because I spoke good English and could just blend in.

I do remember feeling hurt when I checked in at the Townsville airport and went through security. I had an afro comb, the big Islander type. The security ladies looked at each other and smirked. I wished I had it in me to say something to show how proud I was of who I was and that I didn't feel hurt by their action. That was the first time I felt different, but I didn't let it deter me.

My basketball resume includes playing state league, national league and tours to the United States and Canada, and coaching an Indigenous women's team in state league and national championships.

In 1988, after touring with the Indigenous Australian team to Canada and the west coast of the USA, which involved many great experiences, I felt confident to try out for a Women's National Basketball League team, the Lady Bullets. But when I approached them, I was told that north Queensland players were not as good as south Queensland players, so I shouldn't bother.

I was determined to try out: I didn't want to look back and wonder 'what if'. I had nothing to lose: even if I didn't make the squad, at least I would have tried. Thankfully, I made the team. I spent a year in Brisbane and my work back home, QTV, allowed me to take leave without pay.

After I had finished playing at a high level, I was approached to be an assistant coach for a state junior team. This continued for many years, and I also coached the inaugural Kuiyam Pride women's team in the Queensland state competition – the first Indigenous team in a mainstream league.

Because I wasn't married and didn't have a family of my own, I started to look at challenging myself to coach at a higher level, possibly as head coach of a state team or assistant coach in a WNBL team. All that stopped when I had my daughter, Patrina, in 2002. I loved being a mother and a parent; nothing was as important as my daughter. Although my own mother passed away when I was about twenty-three years old, I felt she had taught me a lot. She had shown me how to be independent so that I could live a good life and have a future without her. Maybe that's why Mum was strict and always 'ditri', meaning she was always nagging me to do things: making sure bills were paid, groceries were bought and the house was clean. I still miss her, but I am so thankful for all that she taught me. This is something I do for my own daughter. It's important to be independent, to make good choices, but also to know that failing is part of the process. Most importantly, to always acknowledge where your family is from – the Torres Strait.

I spent two years on Thursday Island. An opportunity to work at the *Torres News* newspaper came up and I knew I couldn't turn that down. I had worked in radio and television for many years, so learning how to write stories was my next challenge. It was an opportunity to take my daughter to the Torres Strait, to see what it's like to live in a remote community. We take things for granted down south and should appreciate what we have. We could always google the Torres Strait and see what it's like, but to actually live there was a great educational experience. I wanted her to meet her family like I had when Mum took us to Thursday Island. The strong connection I have with my cousins is because of Mum taking us to visit family. We'd take the trip around Christmas time and would be there for New Year's and do the powder play with everyone. Thinking about that makes me smile. Great memories.

So when my daughter and I moved to Thursday Island in 2009, it was so she could make some memories with our family, with her school friends and with the wider community. She was lucky to go camping, and to travel with me to Mabuiag Island for work and go fishing in a dinghy around the island.

Maybe the visits to Thursday Island when I was little was a way my mother could keep us connected. I wanted that too for my daughter: to feel connected, to know that's our identity, to be proud of who we are, and to know that we are rich in our culture as Torres Strait Islander people. During NAIDOC celebrations at school, she'd be involved with the cooking and dancing.

Patrina loves to cook and she's better than me at making semur chicken, coconut curry chicken and pakalolo, just to name a few. I've taken her to feastings and tombstone unveilings, to watch island dancing, to church services and the Coming of the Light, and to learn some of the protocols we have during loss or when spending time with in-laws. She understands kriole and can say a few words but not actually have a conversation. I'm happy where she's at in her life, and glad that she can confidently and proudly move in two worlds.

If I were to reflect again on my parents' shift to live and work down south, it was a total transformation of their lives, from what they had known growing up to the complete unknown. If what motivated them was their children and what they wanted for us as a family, I'd say they'd be happy with how my sister Patricia and I are today – confidently and proudly moving in two worlds.

Every time I go to Thursday Island, I enjoy the aerial view from the plane, the bus ride from Horn Island airport to the wharf, soaking up the sight of the beautiful aqua saltwater and enjoying the ferry ride over to the island. It's worse when leaving, always feeling sad as the ferry leaves the wharf.

So with deep sadness, I know my parents would have been homesick many times. They never returned to their homelands of Erub, Mer and Kubin. They made the mainland their home.

Their sacrifice for us is what keeps me going. When I feel down or when things aren't going my way, I always remember how hard it would have been for my parents. They have been my motivation to do well, to excel and to be the best I could be.

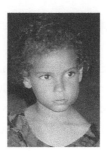

## Two Different Worlds

### Tahlia Bowie

The warmth of the sun, the sea breeze, the laughter and the strong sense of culture and community are just some of the many things that I miss about the Torres Strait whenever I leave.

It has been thirteen years since I moved away from home. I grew up as a child on both Hammond Island and Thursday Island. Life on the islands was extremely laid back, and it still is. I lived on Hammond Island until I was about nine years old. I attended the only primary school on the island until I transitioned into Year 3. From then on, my twin sister and I had to catch a ferry to and from school on Thursday Island, as the primary school campus on Hammond Island only went up to Year 2.

Our family relocated to Thursday Island when I was nine years old. Every weekend we would travel to Hammond Island to be with my great-grandmother. As kids, my sister, my cousins and I would play in our great-grandmother's yard, building cubby houses and raking up the leaves and mango seeds that fell from the many mango trees. She also had a tamarind tree, a star-fruit tree and a few others.

The transition into high school on Thursday Island was fairly easy, as we had friends and relatives attending the same school. We settled in well and participated in many activities, including basketball, volleyball, athletics, dance and music. Everything seemed normal, easygoing and familiar.

In 2008, my great-grandmother passed away at the age of ninety. This would be the beginning of many challenging times in my teen years. The following year, my family and I made the move to Cairns. In my eyes, Cairns was the big smoke. Coming from an island, it seemed that way. But I had no idea about the culture shock I was in for. I expected to settle in quickly, make a lot of friends and kill it both academically and in my extracurricular activities.

The first morning our mother dropped us off at the entrance to our new school, I could feel the major shift and turned around to watch Mum drive away. In moments like this I am grateful to have a twin; at least I wasn't alone. The two of us instantly felt out of place. Compared with our school on Thursday Island, our new school had triple the number of students, bigger buildings, formal school attire and was 90 per cent white. For the first time, I really understood what being a minority felt like. We received a lot of questions about our hair, our accent and where we were from. When we said 'The Torres Strait', most students had no idea where that was … and it's less than a two-hour flight from Cairns.

Almost everything was confronting. At the high school on Thursday Island, my sister and I were in the top maths class. Our maths class in Cairns had so many students that some had to sit on the floor. And to add to our horror, we instantly dropped to the lower maths class. The top class was so advanced, I felt like I had missed a year of school. I would later understand that Thursday Island and Cairns had different systems – and not exactly the same resources.

I would have to explain to my peers that English was my second language when they pointed out my island accent, which still hasn't faded. I often explained the significance of the Torres Strait Islander flag, and that the symbol in the centre of the flag was not a horseshoe but a traditional headdress (dhari, dari or dhoeri). Once, I had to stand in front of the whole year and read a speech for NAIDOC week. As soon as I finished, before I had taken my seat, a friend sitting a couple of seats away said, 'You sound so black.' He was one of the few Aboriginal students in my grade: there were only six of us Indigenous kids in the whole year. I laughed at his comment. I mean, I only know how to be black. I guess the contrast was funny to him too, in that moment, in a predominantly white school. I found it hilarious.

I remember showing a friend of mine my favourite childhood book, *Gelam: The Man from Moa*, a traditional Torres Strait story. The story blew her mind, she had so many questions – especially about the dhogai (witch). I had fun describing that to her. Another topic that arose more than once was the food we ate. My friend was particularly horrified when I told her that the meat I was eating with rice for lunch was dugong meat.

'They are the cutest animals. Why would you eat them?' she asked.

'A dugong is a sea cow. You eat land cow. Same thing!' I replied.

I went on to explain that my ancestors and my community to this day live and survive off the sea. It didn't make her feel any better when I revealed that we also eat turtles.

The original plan was for me and my sister to finish Year 10 and 11 in Cairns and then return home to Thursday Island to graduate with our friends and relatives. Instead, we just stayed and graduated in Cairns. I regret not going home to graduate with friends I'd known for years. I felt like my graduation and formal events were not that significant in Cairns. I was graduating at a school without many memories to cherish. A sense of culture and community was missing. I was finishing off my schooling with people I didn't really know. But I am so grateful for the few special connections I had with some of my classmates. I had a really small circle of friends. Papua New Guinean, Fijian, Aboriginal, Māori and one white girl. It made sense that we gravitated towards each other and felt a connection.

At the age of eighteen, my sister and I made the big move to Sydney. Even further away from home. We weren't afraid. We were young, excited and ready to leave the laid-back pace of Far North Queensland. Sydney opened my eyes to so many things. The many different cultures in the world and different ways of life. It was a busier, faster and bigger environment.

My sister and I figured out that the further we are from home, the more likely it is that people won't know where or what the Torres Strait is. Many people thought the Torres Strait was a whole other country or asked if we needed passports to go there. We struggled to find ways to feel closer to home and to stay connected while living in a place that was the complete opposite. Island songs and cooking island food (simur chicken, sop sop, sabi rice and good old tin-meat stew) in our western Sydney apartment was how we hung on to our culture.

One thing that caught our eye was the fashion. We had never heard of high-end or luxury fashion. In our school years all we wore were baggy shirts, basketball or football shorts and thongs. In Sydney, exposure to the many trends of fashion enticed the two of us to start experimenting. Ultimately, we wanted to wear clothes that would represent our culture and where we were from. The options were very limited, so we had an idea to start our own fashion label.

I had been working in a clothing store, Zara, and studying a styling course online while my sister studied styling and business too. We loved streetwear fashion, so we decided to create a streetwear label that featured Torres Strait Islander designs and influences. We began working on Bowie Empire.

Our clothing label has since opened so many doors for us. We have participated in fashion shows, been featured in magazines like *GQ* and more. But most importantly it has opened conversations about the Torres Strait. We have been able to spread awareness about our home and our culture, and to have Torres Strait Islander people wear our garments proudly is such a heartwarming and humbling feeling. Today, we continue expanding our label here in Brisbane.

I could travel as far as I want to and spend time experiencing new things. However, nothing will ever top sitting on the beach at home, eating mangoes and feeling the sea breeze against my face. No matter where I go or who I meet, I will always be honoured to introduce myself as a proud Torres Strait Islander – Kulkalgal and Maluilgal Nation.

# *Duality*

## Aaliyah-Jade Bradbury

I love the quiet that the sea brings. The lulls of its steady rhythm, the coos of the winds breaking against it. It's meditative – sacred. I often think about the duality of it, about how the sea is constantly changing but remains the same sea my ancestors have sailed on, fished from and grown from for thousands of years.

Growing up, my mother always brought me to the beach when I was mucking up or feeling sad. She often remarked how a day at the beach seemed to wash away any worries I had. It was like the ocean water seeped into my skin and worked its way to the parts of myself that got scared, clearing the fear from my being. My mother explained it as reconnecting with your source. As Indigenous people, we are spiritually tied to sea and country; if we are away from them long enough, parts of our spirit get tired and become lost.

See, I am a second-generation Torres Strait Islander born in Sydney. I have never been to Erub (Darnley Island). I have never known my culture on my country. I have never heard the sounds of the warup being played under Meriam skies. I have never felt how the Erub sands shift under my feet as I dance a kab kar. However, I have heard the warup being played under the roof of the Aboriginal Dance Theatre Redfern. I have felt the hard smoothness of church floors as I kab kar for my cousin's first shave. I may not have known my culture on my country, but I have known it through my community and family.

I knew my upbringing was different from those who grew up in the islands or in Queensland, but I was never made to feel as if that were a bad thing. That was until I went to Bamaga for the first time as a child. I was a long way from Sydney. Where Sydney had cold cement paths, Bamaga had hot red dirt. The air tasted different, thick with humidity and the promise of rain. Kids walked together down the road as camp dogs followed them in hopes of adventure and food. The calls of their Akas as they growled at them to 'hurry up one'. The rhythm of Bamaga was foreign to me, and it was one that I both adored and was heartbroken by. It was the first time I discovered I was different.

I was playing with some other children, who were around my age – that small piknini age when our bellies were still chubby and our laughs still had that twinkle. We played in the yard of my grandfather's property, climbing trees and being a nuisance. I relished the freedom in how we played. But, as I played and joked with them, my world seemed to tilt from its axis in seconds when one of my mother's siblings told me I was white.

I had never been called that before. It confused me to be told I was something I clearly wasn't. My skin is brown, my hair is dark and I had that Reuben smile. I had always seen myself as Blak, my dad a proud Larrakia man from Darwin and my mother a proud Erub woman. I grew up in Redfern with kids like me, where black came in many shades. So you can probably understand my confusion. My family, who had just been giving me so much joy, were now the reason for my tears. Their insistence on my 'whiteness' drove me to the comfort of my mother's arms. Frustrated and bewildered, she rubbed my back, trying to ease me of a pain I couldn't articulate. Bless, my mother gave them a good growling, but the damage was done. I was now the little girl that was not Torres Strait Islander enough.

You can imagine my surprise when, a few years later, I discovered I was too Torres Strait Islander for my Aboriginal family. I had gone up to Darwin for the school holidays. I loved Darwin and still do. I love the wall of humidity that hits you as you leave the airport, laksas for breakfast and, best of all, being on country – my country. I love how my skin seems to glow, and my hair seems to thrive in the heat. I'm made for that country, but my Aboriginal family saw it a bit differently.

My family was celebrating Territory Day. We had come together to feast on fresh crab, adobo and barbeque. The men sat at the back, drinking their beers, while the women enjoyed the cold comfort of the air-conditioned lounge room. My cousins and I did what every other Territory kid did and ran wild with sparklers in our hands. We thought we were wizards. It was a genuinely magical night for me.

My cousin Nene had invited her next-door neighbours to play with us, a girl and a boy. The girl was taller than us, with long straight hair and bright-pink sandals. She looked at me, confused.

'Why do you look like that?' she said.

'What do you mean?' I replied.

'I thought you were Nene's cousin?' she examined pointedly.

I looked at her and then at Nene, my eyes pleading for some backup.

Nene sighed and rolled her eyes. 'It's cause her mum is Torres Strait Islander.'

The girl eased. 'Oh, so that's why you look like that. You're not Aboriginal. You're not a proper Cubillo.'

My stomach sank, and I felt myself shrink again. My cousin didn't defend me, but she confirmed that I was tainted because of my Torres Strait Islander heritage – somehow not worthy of my Aboriginality. So I found myself in that weird position again. To the people around me, I was neither.

As I grew and matured, I began a complicated, almost paradoxical, relationship with my identity. A dance of contradictions. I had learnt to be a chameleon, being who people expected me to be, all because I didn't feel like I truly belonged. But identity is a lot like growing up. There are growing pains. The person you were is not always the person you become. It takes time. Looking back at these moments as an adult, I understand them differently now. I look at them with kinder eyes.

I look back at my visit to Bamaga as a time not defined by my family calling me white but by the warm vibrancy of a Torres Strait Islander household. The type of household where the old people will growl at you and give you the biggest hugs. Where the smells of damper permeate the air and leave your belly hungry. The way the room goes quiet when we pray before eating. The way jokes are to be made at every opportunity just to make those old women do an 'aunty' laugh – the gut-sore kind. The way the night fills with the bright sounds of reggae. It was paradise. A Shangri-La. I belonged there.

I reflect on my time in Darwin and remember how my uncle soothed my heart. He reminded me that I was both Aboriginal and Torres Strait Islander, and even though he was an Aboriginal man he could speak Yumplatok. He had learned Torres Strait culture while learning Indigenous dance in Sydney. He made me feel like there was room for me in my family.

It is a beautiful thing being Torres Strait Islander, and I am forever thankful to experience the privilege of my identity. My culture is made up of love, passion and the spirit of our ancestors. And even though I may not be connected in the ways that other Torres Strait Islanders are, I know that I am blessed. It's like the sea. My culture is continuously changing, but it remains the same culture my ancestors had for thousands of years. And just like the sea, my culture is my life force. It's sacred.

# Complexion

## Sorren Thomas

Seingapa maiem, my name is Sorren, and through my mother I am a proud Torres Strait Islander woman. I was raised by my mother, Katherine (Kitty) Abednego, whose family descend from the Mualgal people of Moa Island. My athe's and aka's names were Koko and Napiau Abednego.

Before I begin, I'd like to thank you for reading my story and those written alongside it in the pages of this book. I'm grateful to have the opportunity to be heard, though the exposure and immortalisation of my words is frightening. I urge you to be kind; I'm about to share with you not only the narrative of my journey thus far, but also the insecurities that plagued my childhood and adolescence, which I've not shared with many. As I've gone on to forgive my younger self for the unfair thoughts which almost defined me, I hope you can show me patience in reading them.

I was born in Rockhampton on Darumbal Country and raised by my single mother with my five older brothers. My mother was born on Thursday Island and moved with her family to mainland Australia when she was seven years old. She was raised in Townsville, where she attended school until Year 10, at which point she left school to begin work to assist in supporting her family. My biological father was absent from my life. I met him only a handful of times as a child, and he played no role in my upbringing.

My family and I lived in government housing at the end of a relatively secluded suburban street. The house itself was a small, single-floor brick house whose mortar had cracked in areas, exposing little slithers of the outside world to our interior dwelling. The house had three small bedrooms: one for my mother, one for me and the other split for two of my brothers. The garage was converted into a bedroom for the remaining boys, who consequently shared their 'private' space with our hot-water system and washing machine. We shared one small bathroom between us, and shower times and hot water use were always a point of conflict.

As you may suspect, our family did not enjoy the financial comfort which often (though not always) accompanies a two-income household. My mother had five mouths to feed (my eldest brother was old enough to live elsewhere) and five bodies to dress, and she did so independently without a cent of child support. My brothers and I would get ourselves home from school while my mother remained at work until the late afternoon, and the household chores were divided between us. We each cleaned one shared room of the house, rotating each week to keep things fair. This was necessary to lift some of the household burden from my mother, but also to teach us discipline and responsibility. After returning home from work, my mother would begin preparing dinner for us all. After we had eaten, it was the role of my brothers and I to clean the dishes. One of us would be allocated to washing, another to drying and putting away. I wish I could tell you these arrangements went as smoothly as they sound, but there were very often arguments over fairness or 'quality'. Recalling all of this, I look back on those years with the utmost warmth in my heart and a smile on my face; hell hath no fury like a sibling allocated more chores than another.

I always knew I was a Torres Strait Islander gel; my mother spoke Creole at home and taught us protocol. She would cook us traditional dishes, and we would often travel north to Townsville for family reunions and events. As a child, my identity was never in question, and I never had to answer for it. Although, it was obvious that my brothers and I were different from our cousins. My father was a koleh man, so my brothers and I quite literally come in varying shades. I am fair-skinned with wavy brunette hair, and my mother is brown-skinned with curly black hair. These were the features that I felt were missing in me. It's important I tell you this so you can understand my inner conflict as a child and adolescent.

As I've mentioned, my mother worked full time and continues to do so to this day. This meant that I attended day care most days of the week until I began primary school. This wasn't a bad thing, nor was it unique. I developed social skills and got to enjoy the creative activities put on for our busy little minds. That said, it was also the first time my identity was questioned. One day, another little girl asked me: 'Is that really your mum? Why is she black?'

I don't remember the girl's name, but she was just an innocent child who, like me, grew up in a markedly less progressive, less accepting Australia. The question itself wasn't overly unsettling, but the derogatory connotation with which she emphasised the final word crushed me. Indigenous people did not have even a fraction of the recognition or respect that we do now. Racism and cruel stereotypes were so grossly normalised for my generation, although it's inexcusable regardless of the times. They had not touched me until that day, and at three years old the shame of her words burned so deep into my consciousness that I was lost in myself and my cultural identity for years. Of course that was my mother; how dare you speak of the woman who gave me life with a tone of disapproval? How dare you invalidate me as her daughter because of the colour of my skin? I wish I could have whispered an affirmation or two to little Sorren on that day, given her a cuddle and guided her gently away. Likewise, I wish I could have explained the impact words can have to this little koleh girl, tell her it's normal to be curious, and perhaps give her an explanation to her question. But I was just my three-year-old self, unprepared for the situation and confused by its implications. Did I have to be brown-skinned to be my mother's daughter? Did that mean I had to be brown-skinned to be Torres Strait Islander?

I developed a shame for not looking how I *thought* I was supposed to look. Later that day, I asked my mother if the contrast between our complexions mattered, probing directly to ask if I had come from her belly. I recall my attempt to seem casual and unconcerned, though, truthfully, I was nervous that there was even a slight chance I wasn't her daughter. She assured me (on more than one occasion) that I was irrefutably her child, and when I consider our mutual short temper and offensively loud laugh I'm convinced beyond a shadow of a doubt. With one half of my new-found identity crisis negated, I now had the remainder of my childhood, adolescence and young adult life to contend with the other. Back then, my features were unworthy of the culture with which I so tenderly identified, and it took me years to understand that the insecurity surrounding my identity was rooted far deeper than at the level of my skin.

I was the only Torres Strait Islander student at my primary school (my brothers were now in high school) and received many comments about the legitimacy of my Indigenous status. Each time they stemmed from childish curiosity but carried a subtle judgement. I was often referred to as a 'half-caste' and asked what percentage of Torres Strait Islander blood I carried. The emotional burden of navigating these conversations as a child only reinforced my self-doubts; I was ashamed that I had to validate myself and conscious that it was owing to my fairer skin tone. I was anxious that I would eventually encounter someone who either completely rejected my claim to Torres Strait Islander heritage or held spiteful views toward Indigenous people. Ultimately this was inevitable, with one child going so far as to ask if I was relieved to have light skin, because 'black people are dirty and drink all day, you're lucky you get to live off all the black benefits but not look it'.

I realise now as an adult that this child likely didn't intend to offend me, and the nonchalant racism they had introduced to our otherwise harmless, childish conversation was not an opinion of their own construct. Rather, their words were a regurgitation, a reflection of the environment in which they were raised. I wish I could tell you I took the high road and righteously educated this child for their blatantly racist comment and we then proceeded to enjoy our recess in harmony. But I was nine years old and fiercely defensive of my family. I violently shoved them to the ground and watched in disgust as they ran from me, crying. Surprisingly, they didn't mention it to a teacher. I assumed it was because they realised the venom in their words was harmful and untrue, and I hope they've never let it seep from their mouth again.

As I grew older, the centre of my fears shifted from whether I was truly Torres Strait Islander to whether I was Torres Strait Islander *enough*. The doubts of others were my greatest fear, because my own conviction was so fragile. While I was raised to be assertive and, in my heart, I knew I was Torres Strait Islander, I became increasingly aware of the gaps in my cultural knowledge. The beauty of the Torres Strait Islander people is that our identity is at both a macro and micro level. Macro in that we are all Torres Strait Islanders, micro in that we come from different islands, all with unique customs and language. Having been born on mainland Australia, I was not raised in the same culture as those born and raised on island, I do not have the same ties to native land or knowledge of language and custom. I do not know the traditional way of living in the Torres Strait; I did not learn the songs and dances, or hear the stories passed down by word of mouth. Coupled with my antipathy toward the shade of my skin, I harboured shame and disappointment at how very little I knew about the culture that I held so dear. I felt that I could not belong anywhere; I was detached from Zenadth Kes and too ethnic for my koleh friends. How very lonely it was back then to be mixed race. I was scared to reach out, fearing denial, and scared to ask questions, fearing retribution.

My primary school education was devoid of Indigenous history. The atrocities against the Stolen Generations were not included in our curriculum. I didn't understand colonisation, the extent of the genocide which devastated the Aboriginal people was beyond me until I reached high school; only then was it uncovered at my own personal finding. By the same token, I was also never taught of the history of Torres Strait Islanders; we never discussed what the Torres Strait was, Islanders' story of colonisation or how we differed from Aboriginal peoples. To be blunt, Torres Strait Islanders have never been mentioned in any classroom or any lecture I have ever attended to this day. While our educational institutions have failed me by neglecting my culture – one of the two cultures composing the Indigenous roots of this nation – they have also failed non-Indigenous students, who are ignorant to the true history of this country and the implications of the trauma left in the wake of its colonisation.

It was an incredibly confusing, frustrating time in my life. Awareness of Torres Strait Islanders was (and still is throughout much of Australia) extremely limited, and under-representation is unfortunately still quite common. Realistically, I was limited in my ability to share and educate about Torres Strait Islander culture, but I was also never asked. Once I entered university, I was only ever invited to give my perspective on Aboriginal culture and experience as the only Indigenous student in the room. When I would clarify that my Torres Strait Islander culture was entirely distinct from Aboriginal culture and so I could not speak on these issues, their heads would turn away and I was again just another student with nothing to contribute. I was a token Indigenous student until it was discovered that I was the *wrong kind* of Indigenous. There is a unique pain growing up as a mixed-race child, and that pain is compounded when one of your cultures is often ignored.

There was no interest in my people; not once did anyone ask me to explain the difference or shed light on my background. When not even the history of the traditional custodians of the land on which we were learning was being taught, is it surprising attention was never turned to the Torres Strait Islands? It wasn't appropriate; more work was needed before there would be a chance to discuss Zenadth Kes. However, even if there *had* been such a chance, I was so riddled with self-criticism of my own identity that I wouldn't have had the strength to participate in those conversations.

In lieu of any interest in my Islander culture, the questions I did receive, if they weren't querying my Indigenous legitimacy, explored the depth of the assistance schemes allegedly at my disposal. Friends would sooner ask me how much financial assistance I received from Centrelink than hear stories about my culture. 'Yes bala, it's more than you – it took twice the work and sacrifice you couldn't possibly comprehend to be here at the same place.'

It's a shame I spent so many years of my youth resisting the urge to truly lean into my culture for fear of rejection. I was caught between my ailan spirit, pulling me to reconnect and advocate for my people, and my fear of denial owing to my mainland heritage and fair skin.

Despite the walls I put up to protect myself from anticipated ostracism, I have always had a deep love for my Torres Strait Islander roots. The very first moment I heard the beat of the warup and rhythm of the thrum as a child, it was like a breath of fresh air. I was overcome by both awe and pride, and hearing our songs and instruments will always fill my spiritual cup.

I appreciate your patience thus far; I hope I've not conveyed an insufferable sense of self-pity. This was simply my lived experience, and in truth I was far too harsh on my younger self – I knew more about my cultural protocol and language than I gave myself credit for. Regardless, as an adult I'm thankful for the desire to learn more, as it has guided me to delve deeper into the history of my people that is scarcely recognised.

It's a blessing to belong to a culture; to have customs and history, songs and dance that tell the stories of ancient traditions from which you may draw strength. Being a Torres Strait Islander woman is one of my many blessings, one that I will never question again. As I write my story now, I can assure you the insecurities that once loomed over me as a child are gone, and as I've gained more confidence in myself and in my cultural identity, I'm attempting to point out the under-representation of my people when I can. The voices of Indigenous peoples over the years have called for recognition and, slowly but surely, they are being heard. And now mine is too, kaima esso for listening.

Culture and adversity influenced my childhood, and looking back I am forever thankful to be touched by both. I am thankful for the authors who have written the history and lore of my people, strengthening both my cultural knowledge and my pride. I am thankful for the publishers and editors of *Growing Up Torres Strait Islander in Australia* for giving me the opportunity to share with you all, and to reflect on how far I've grown both spiritually and emotionally. Likewise, I'm immensely proud of my family and our story. There's nowhere on this earth I would rather have grown up than as a Torres Strait Islander girl with my family, at the end of our quiet street, in our little brick house.

During one discussion with my beloved aunty, Annie Gela – recognised Elder and traditional artist – to learn of my roots while visiting home, she affirmed to me one of her quotes, which still resonates with me deeply:

> Culture and Language stand together like strong pillars supporting the intrinsic part of a person's soul. If a person gains even the basic knowledge and understanding of one or the other, it will give one great courage and strength to stand alone and identify themselves to their race of people without hesitation.

# The Big
# *Wongai Tree*

**Daniella Williams**

Every afternoon after school, Sissy always walk about gor for em Nene and Dato house for play until em mum and dad e finish from work. Favourite thing blo em for do e climb up the big wongai tree front where em Nene and Dato house.

Sometimes em make em wasseh cubby house, carry all short piece of wood and laydown em across all branch for makeh all chair for sidown. If not em gor act for be inside circus ah swing from branch to branch try legor all tricks. Nor more hang upside down wasseh sapurr.

But this one day em be gor for em Nene and Dato house, em be pretend the big wongai tree be em pirate ship. So em be gor find eh one toilet paper roll for use em wasseh em pirate spyglass and em be also grab one plastic bag so em can tie em up em wasseh em pirate flag.

That same day e look be nother kind windy. But em still legor strong ed for climb up the big wongai tree for play.

There em start climb up the big wongai tree, em Dato be there sidown where the front door for sea breeze. Em Dato allah for em, "AY YOU NOR CLIMB UP THE TREE, YOU LOOK E WINDY?!"

But Sissy still climb up and allah gor byk for em Dato, "WAH, I SABEH. I GOR BE CAREFUL."

Sissy end up climb up gor right untup for the top so em can tie em up the plastic bag wasseh em pirate flag. While em tie em up the plastic bag em hook eh em leg gor round the tree tight one so em can't fall down. The wind e wasseh come more strong now. But em still play there right untup.

Em there now act for look through em pirate spyglass where the toilet paper roll. No more allah, "GOR LEFT E GUD STONE YA FRONT!"

Then all of sudden one mina kind big wind be blow. Sissy matha looseh grip ah falldown come down. But lucky em be hit all branch before em be hit the ground for break em fall.

There em hit the ground em be land lor em right side. Em busseh nother kind big cry ah hold em right side arm.

Em Dato onetime run down the stairs blo house ah rip em singlet where same speed.

There em Dato kesem where em, em spik for em, "LOOK! WANEM I BE SPIK YOU? NOR CLIMB UP THE TREE, E WINDY!"

Then em Dato gor grab the broken singlet and tie em up em where Sissy right arm ah makeh sling.

Em Dato gor allah for em Nene for grab eh the car key and nother singlet so them two can takeh Sissy gor hospital.

But when the doctor be check Sissy, lucky em nor be brokeh bone. E be kasa sprained.

But from that day on Sissy be learn eh lesson…
"LISTEN TALK BUMBI ACCIDENT"

This story is dedicated to my Granny
and Grandad Majid xo

# *Thriving Spaces*

## Jaqui Hughes

I love being a doctor. It's been a professional identity I have associated myself with since high school. My grandmother gifted me the blessing of being a doctor – that is, she invited me to share that part of her identity, since she was a doctor who had a long and important career, serving the people of the Northern Territory across many speciality and leadership roles.

My family encouraged me, gave me opportunities and supported me. Growing up, I loved making things that were needed. I sewed school uniforms for my sisters, I cultivated an amazing veggie garden, I baked. My older sister, among her many talents, was a beautiful singer, and we sang songs in harmony and put on musicals for our family in the school holidays.

We also played hockey. I was strong as an inner or halfback, supporting the flow of the ball from defence to attack. We were a family of six girls, and there would be one of my sisters involved in most passes, either saving goals or scoring. Playing with my sisters was always special, cheering each other on and celebrating each other's technical skill and endurance, our fitness and our on-field focus. We were the Whap girls. With six of us, we supported many years of premiership success for our local hockey team, and my sisters did very well at representative-level sport.

I thrived at school and responded well to my family's encouragement. I liked doing well academically, since to study medicine at university like my grandma I would need good grades. English was a subject I really enjoyed. It has been a skill that continues to serve me well, expressing myself verbally and in writing, at university and later in my professional career and creative life.

So I'm an older daughter from a big family, I communicate well and negotiate well, and I enjoy designing and making things. I use all these skills as an entrepreneurial doctor – I learn from people about their health and wellness needs, locate and provide the healthcare they need and create that care if it does not yet exist.

As a Torres Strait Islander, I am the first in my field – the first Aboriginal or Torres Strait Islander specialist doctor in renal medicine in Australia. Kidneys are important for all the body systems, and many Aboriginal and Torres Strait Islander people know someone or have a family member who has had kidney disease or needed dialysis. Kidney health is important in my Zenadh (Torres Strait) family too.

Even though I have been first in my field in a professional sense, I have never been without wisdom and support from the people who wanted me to do well. Mum always believed in me, and I remember her encouragement as a young girl. Aunties showed me how to do well when I was studying interstate at uni. Grandma mentored me in navigating medical practice, and my Zenadh family mentored me in using my leadership to provide health care in the way that our people need. All my family elders, who are knowledge and wisdom holders (my sisters, parents, grandma, aunts and uncles), passed forward their skills so that I could gain the mastery, eldership and purpose that have upheld my role as a healthcare professional.

That privilege comes with an important cultural responsibility. My work contributes to increasing the longlife of our people. 'Longlife' is a term that can literally mean old age, like an athe or aka (grandfather or grandmother), but also a spiritual long life. It is beautiful knowing that our people thrived in our country for thousands of years, and that we know where we come from and whom we belong to. More recently, chronic illnesses such as diabetes and kidney disease have altered the longlife of Zenadh families. Our cultural health has always been part of our health and our longlife, yet this has only recently been recognised by universities and healthcare services. The people of Zenadh stand tall in culture. So too, health professionals of Zenadh, stand tall in Culture and mobilise your wisdom with love for our people to regain our heritage – the longlife which has always been known by past elders.

## Thriving spaces: three poems

### SURVIVING

Our body knows longlife
Yet near time was drained
Building the strength
Refilling the time
Standing in power
longlife regained

## NAVIGATING

I was scribing a meeting
Standing he pointed
Asked the room who I was
'I am meant to be here'
That settled it, man
Sit down and consider
Your thinking's a problem
Longlife still to gain

## THRIVING

Kindness in friends
Family supported
Community are near
A hug and a cheer
Peace with the quiet
Known in the space
Standing in power
Cared for by grace

These poems reveal spaces I have visited and dwelt in, either for some or lots of time, in the day-to-day of growing up, grounding within and standing tall, known and loved as Oman of Wagadagam.

The second poem, 'Navigating', is a specific recollection of managing an unanticipated harm, and of being denied a sense of belonging in a place that should be ours to legitimately dwell in. In that moment, for me, that legitimacy was aligned to the purpose described in the first poem, 'Surviving'. The incident occurred some time past, but I put it into words in 2019. It was an incredibly hurtful experience, being overtly questioned in a space that should have offered all people respect.

Recovery from those harms is offered in the third poem, 'Thriving'. Thriving in the day-to-day means restoring, rejuvenating and healing through the precious relationships one has with other people. It means the acceptance and celebration of being, just because we are.

# The Ties That Bind

## Adam C. Lees

I am a terrible example of a Torres Strait Islander. I don't like seafood and will always order a sizzling, fat, juicy sirloin steak over a piece of snapper. Embarrassingly, I have never caught a fish, and at my age I am unlikely to adopt recreational angling as a hobby anytime soon. Moreover, I've never cracked a coconut or climbed a tree to collect one. Instead, I cook with tinned coconut cream.

I didn't grow up learning to speak any traditional Torres Strait languages, including my ancestral tongue, Miriam Mir, but I can understand some Kriol or Yumplatok, a form of pidgin English that has become an everyday language of the Torres Strait and parts of Cape York. Growing up, I wasn't taught any traditional songs or dances; this is a tragedy, because my great-grandfather Victor Blanco and great-uncle George Blanco performed kab kar, a traditional form of Torres Strait Islander dance, before King George IV and Queen Elizabeth II, respectively.

Regarding my physical appearance, I've become accustomed to seeing a tidal wave of disappointment wash over people's faces because I don't meet their mental image or expectation of who or what a Torres Strait Islander should be; I'm the opposite. I'm fair-skinned and have green eyes and straight brown hair. I have a bulbous nose and often wonder which side of the family I inherited it from, but it would be brave of me to claim this as a Torres Strait Islander feature. Size-wise, I feel at home and blend in when I visit the Torres Strait. Like many of my countrymen, I am a Hulk with a large build. I am six foot three, have enormous hands and wear a size-fourteen shoe. On my last visit to the Torres Strait, a family member began comparing our body sizes and builds. Looking me up and down, he told me that I looked like an FBI.

'As in a federal police officer?' I asked.

'No, a fucking big Islander,' he joked.

We both laughed. I hadn't heard that line before.

Don't get me wrong. I would love to perform traditional dance, fish and speak my ancestral tongue, because these should be the cultural hallmarks of any Torres Strait Islander. However, my upbringing was different. Like many Torres Strait Islanders today, I was born on the mainland. My story began in Queanbeyan, New South Wales, in May 1972. One of four children, I am an Australian of Torres Strait Islander, Aboriginal, Filipino, English and Irish ancestry. Through my mum's side, I descend from the Meriam people of Mer or Murray Island in the Eastern Torres Strait, some 120 kilometres from the tip of Cape York. I am connected to the Magaram and Teg Dauareb clans, and our totems include the snake (Tabo), whale (Galbol), mackerel (Dabor), dolphin (Bid), dugong (Deger) and the fruit dove (Dibadiba). Through my second great-grandmother, Annie

Blanco, I also descend from the Yadhaigana, a seafaring Aboriginal people from the eastern side of Cape York Peninsula.

Rather than by the magnificent turquoise and azure waters of the tropical Torres Strait, I was raised in the prosperous but remote mining city of Mount Isa in far north-west Queensland. My hometown is nestled among the rugged, spinifex-covered hills and deep-red earth of the Selwyn Range, with Townsville, some 900 kilometres to the east, being the closest city.

Our family, including my dad, Terry, mum, Pattie, older sisters, Nyree and Cassie, and younger brother, Matthew, made the long drive from Cairns to Mount Isa in our tanned Kingswood five-door wagon when I was about five years old. Our sausage dog, Gemma, also made the trek. Before that, Dad owned an insurance business in Canberra that went 'belly-up' after a series of financial woes. The bank foreclosed on our family home in Mawson, and we relied on our family's generosity to see us through the hard times. Fortunately, Dad found a permanent job in Mount Isa in 1977 as an area manager and marketing representative with beer, wine and spirit merchants Cummins and Campbell Ltd, a subsidiary of Carlton United Breweries. We have called 'The Isa' home ever since. Growing up in Mount Isa on the traditional lands of the Kalkadoon people, my only understanding of the Torres Strait came from school or other people in the community. And from our tiny three-bedroom fibro home on Buna Street along the banks of the Leichhardt River, the Torres Strait seemed as fantastical as the land of Narnia, made famous by author C.S. Lewis.

Mount Isa's environment is harsh. There is no waking up to the delicate sounds of waves lapping the shore, or to a soft frangipani-scented sea breeze blowing over the Coral Sea and across the Strait. Instead, our throats often tingled from the distinctive taste of sulphur-dioxide fumes from the Mount Isa Mines copper stack. Mount Isa is also scorching hot. It's the type of place where you can fry an egg on the burning concrete pavement during the height of summer. Forget about 'Taba Naba' (a popular Meriam song and sit-down dance about going out to the edge of the reef and fishing). There were no beaches or reefs for us to visit to cool off. Our nearest body of water was Lake Moondarra, a large constructed dam that wasn't safe to swim in because of its frequent duck-lice infestations. There were no Torres Strait pigeons (deumer) or fruit doves (dibadiba) to be found here, but there were plenty of galahs, pelicans, cormorants, cockatoos and peacocks. Back then, some families also enjoyed a swim at Poison Waterhole, a former open-cut copper mine that had been partially filled with water. Now, entering the waterhole is strictly prohibited as the reservoir is part of an area on an active mining lease.

*

Our family ties to the Torres Strait significantly changed about fourteen years before I was born. My mum, her two sisters and two brothers were removed from my grandmother, Agnes (generally known as Aggie), in Cairns in October 1958 and declared wards of the state of Queensland on the grounds of neglect. Mum was just ten. The family was split and sent to different locations. Mum and her brothers, Terry and Michael, were eventually sent by the State Children Department to live on Palm Island Aboriginal Settlement off the coast of Halifax, Queensland; her sisters, Johanne and Elin, were fostered by non-Indigenous families. While in state care, Mum and some of her siblings experienced more than a decade of traumatic sexual, physical and psychological abuse. My mother and I wrote extensively about these experiences in her memoir, *A Question of Colour: My Journey to Belonging* (Magabala Publishing, 2020).

As a family, we continue to experience the traumatic, inter-generational side effects of Mum's removal and separation. It's taken most of my adult life to come to terms with my family history, reconstruct our past, find extended family and thread the interwoven strands of our fractured Torres Strait Islander identity. Unlike most Islanders, I wasn't raised within an extended family environment. There were no family photo albums, just stray photographs. We were excluded from family reunions and special events like weddings and tombstone unveilings because we had been forgotten or relatives didn't know we existed.

Mum often reminds us that we arrived in Mount Isa with the ass out of our pants and no money. I don't recall wearing hand-me-downs or second-hand clothes, but we did. I remember Dad working long hours to provide for us and Mum mostly being the homemaker. We were limited to two-minute hot showers in winter because the hot-water system was unreliable. Mum learnt to cook while working as a kitchenhand in the girls' dormitory on Palm Island; she learnt both traditional and popular Aboriginal and Islander dishes. If Mum didn't serve oven-grilled lamb chops with crispy skin, gravy and mashed potatoes for dinner, it was spaghetti bolognese, cabbage stew with rice, chicken with vermicelli, and regular servings of fried scones with butter and golden syrup. Mum was always good at improvising stews; fish and seafood were never part of our staple diet, except for the occasional serving of deep-frozen Findus-brand fish fingers from a family-sized carton. Like most kids in the Isa and even the Torres Strait, we grew up eating salty plums or dried prunes cured with a sugary, salty liquorice mixture; our fingers were often stained bright red from their colour.

As a family, we were a tight-knit unit. Upon reflection, we had a good upbringing even though our first house was over-crowded. The four kids shared a room with two bunk beds, while mum's younger brother, Uncle Michael, occupied the other bedroom or the couch in our living room. We certainly had a full house when Grandma Aggie came to stay in 1977 when I was five.

According to an African proverb attributed to Amadou Hampâté Bâ, when an elder dies, a library burns to the ground. Such was the case when my grandmother died. Born Temana Agnes Philomena Blanco, Grandma Aggie was born in the vill-age of Gigred on Mer in September 1921. She was the eldest daughter of my great-grandfather Victor Blanco and great-grandmother Azey Leyah Sari, a Miriam woman. Her only sister, Teama ('Tina' or 'Celestina') Blanco, died decades before in Cairns, and her brother, George Blanco, a policeman on Murray Island, had died a few years earlier in 1972.

Over the years, I have learned that my family's migration from the Torres Strait to mainland Australia occurred progres-sively during World War II. Grandma Aggie left Thursday Island for Babinda, North Queensland, with her first husband, Jack Janke, in April 1941, when she was about twenty years old. Other relatives, including my second-great-grandmother, Annie Blanco, great-grandmother, Azey Leyah Sari, and great-aunts Tina and Josephine Blanco, arrived on the mainland in Janu-ary 1942, following the compulsory evacuation of the Thursday Island group under threat from Japanese air raids. They never returned to Torres Strait, although Grandma Aggie had always wanted to. Grandma Aggie divorced her first husband and later remarried. She lived in many places in Far North Queensland, including Babinda, Cairns, Cooktown, Mossman, Daintree and Port Douglas.

Described by everyone who knew her as a woman before her time, Grandma Aggie was known by locals as the first girl on Thursday Island to wear tiny shorts, high heels and make-up. The tales of what Grandma Aggie and her younger sister, Tina, got up to set tongues wagging all over Thursday Island and provided regular fodder among the more gossip-prone residents. She rejected conservative island life and dreamed of a bigger and better life beyond the confines of the Torres Strait. As evidence of her sharp mind and intellect, a district welfare officer from the State Children Department noted in official correspondence in 1958 that 'she is rather a superior type for a coloured woman'.

But by the time she arrived in Mount Isa, there was no trace left of the beautiful, witty, brilliant, convent-educated woman that Grandma Aggie was said to have been. Grandma Aggie's body and mind had become ravaged by decades of alcohol abuse and an aggressive form of cancer that left her bedridden and primarily non-communicative. I remember taking meals to her at dinnertime and the distinct smell of her pills and medications and the little brown bottles in which they were contained. I remember her deep laugh, warm smile and how her face lit up when our dog, Gemma, gave birth to a litter of puppies. She was tall, lean and dark with frizzy hair and high-set cheekbones. I also remember being terrified, screaming out for Mum after seeing Grandma Aggie rushing across the hallway with diarrhea running down her legs, having suffered the indignity of losing bowel control. It was the first time I remember seeing her walk, let alone leave the bed; her body was so thin and skeleton-like. It's a visual that remains seared in my memory.

There were many visits to the Mount Isa Base Hospital when Grandma Aggie's health deteriorated and she entered palliative care. As if it were yesterday, I can visualise stepping out of the slow elevator with the large round buttons and walking down the corridor to her ward. Passing by other patients in bed, I recollect the awfulness of seeing an old man with a missing eye resting upright in his bed, the dark hollow cavity of his left eye on full display. I also remember the sadness and grief that overwhelmed our family when Grandma Aggie died. She was only fifty-seven. I wasn't allowed to attend her funeral because I was too young. But I recall my Aunty Johanne, Uncle Terry and Uncle Michael travelling to Mount Isa for the service. Apart from unrealised dreams and unfulfilled potential, the greatest tragedy of Grandma Aggie's life and passing was that she had only been reunited with Mum and her other children a few years earlier after more than a decade of separation.

Grandma Aggie represented our last direct physical link to the Torres Strait Islands. She was the holder of our family knowledge, the custodian of our connection to the past and the old ways. She was the one with all the stories, the yarns, the anecdotes and the songs. It still feels like we have been finding our place and filling in the blanks ever since.

*

Perhaps because of Mum's upbringing on Palm Island Aboriginal Settlement, I was raised with a solid Aboriginal worldview and consciousness rather than a Torres Strait Islander one. As a kid, I remember attending community gatherings at the Ballyana Hall, a sizeable simple aluminium shed the size of a typical Police Citizens Youth Club (PCYC) hall. It was a place where the local Aboriginal community would hold events and dances. It was also the era of the fight for land rights and equal pay. There was a strong sense of unity and a collective desire to make social progress through activism. Maybe I was naïve and seeing the world through a child's eyes, but we seemed more united as Indigenous peoples then. At that time, it didn't seem to matter where other Murris came from, whether we were Traditional Owners or not or even if we weren't from that region. I grew up witnessing Mum's fierce activism and leadership alongside many prominent local leaders, including Aunty Iris Clay and Eric Kyle, who established the local Aboriginal Legal Service in Mount Isa in the 1970s. It was a time of many civil rights gains, and being at the centre of it was pretty special.

Although Mount Isa was once regarded as the most multicultural city in Australia, with over fifty-two nationalities living and working alongside each other, there weren't many Torres Strait Islander residents in the late 1970s and 1980s. There was the Pigliafiori family, who were of Italian and Torres Strait Islander heritage, and the Wasaga family, Aunty Ruth Kyle and her family, who were of Meriam descent. I only discovered we were related after she died. The Baker family from Erub (Darnley Island) lived down the road in Cloncurry, about an hour's drive east of Mount Isa. Meanwhile, other Islanders lived further away in other cities, including Townsville and Cairns. It's probable that other Torres Strait families came and went; Mount Isa has always been a transient mining community. A decade earlier, there was an influx of about 150 Torres Strait Islander labourers who worked on constructing the Townsville to Mount Isa rail line; the late Eddie Koiki Mabo worked on the line and became involved in trade unionism, representing the Torres Strait Islanders working on the project. Eventually, the Hankin and

Gaulai families moved to town, followed over time by others, including members of the Toby, Charlie and Bin Tahal families and others.

When our mothers socialised, I enjoyed hanging out with the other Aboriginal kids, including the Kings, the Speechleys, and the Duffy and Kyle families. They'd often play card games or attend bingo nights at the Irish Club or Concordia Club. These card tournaments weren't for the weak – they lasted for several days and nights, often without interruption. Bottomless cups of Bushells tea and biscuits sustained everyone. While our mothers gambled, us kids made our own fun, including swimming in the flooded creeks, riding our bikes around the town and just hanging out together. Upon reflection, we were well behaved and didn't engage in too much mischief. Occasionally, Dad used to deliver alcohol to pubs in regional communities such as Dajarra and Boulia. I remember riding with him in a big Mack truck during one of those trips.

I don't recall any specific Torres Strait Islander cultural influence throughout my childhood. Sometimes, Mum would find an old pair of pantyhose, carefully cut the legs off and stuff them with Scrabble tiles. Then, she'd sing and perform parts of the traditional Torres Strait Islander dance Tamini around the house while stomping her feet and shaking the pantyhose legs like a pair of maracas. We used to crack up laughing. The sound of a Scrabble-tile-filled sock is identical to kulaps or gor, the seed-rattle instrument used throughout the Torres Strait in traditional songs and dances. I also remember meeting my cousin Raymond Blanco, a renowned dancer with the National Aboriginal and Islander Skills Development Academy (NAISDA), when he and other performers visited Mount Isa schools under the auspices of the Arts Queensland regional touring program.

I first visited the Torres Strait in 2000, for the annual Torres Strait Cultural Festival. I immediately felt like I had come home. I returned in September 2002 with Mum and my sister Cassie. This time we travelled to Thursday Island to undertake family research and make personal and family connections. During this trip, we had the opportunity to meet prominent local identity and Elder Aunty Flo Kennedy. Aunty Flo was close to my grandmother and was a bridesmaid at her wedding on Thursday Island in 1940. I remember Aunty Flo's first reaction upon seeing me.

'Ah, you are big like your people,' she said.

We chatted with Aunty Flo for several hours at the Jardine Hotel. We had the opportunity to record her memories of family and historical events and her musings about the Torres Strait. She shared them generously. Now and then, I listen to the cassettes from that day and remember our time together.

Although she was unwell then, I also had the opportunity to reconnect with Aunty Rita Mills of the legendary Torres Strait Islander musical trio The Mills Sisters. I first met Aunty Rita and her husband, Brett, when they travelled to Apia, Samoa, as part of the Australian delegation to the Twenty-Sixth Festival of Pacific Arts. Aunty Rita also shared many memories of my grandmother, who used to babysit her and her sisters, Ina and Cessa, when they were younger.

Walking around Thursday Island, I came to appreciate the history and contribution of my Filipino forebearers to the pearling industry and the Torres Strait, including the establishment of Our Lady of the Sacred Heart School, which several generations of my family attended. My second-great-grandfather Juan Blanco arrived in the Torres Strait in the late 1800s from

Kalibo, Capiz, in the Western Visayas region of the Philippines. He was a pearler, and like other Asiatic and Filipino immigrants to Australia at that time, Juan was attracted by the opportunity to be a part of the growing pearl-shell industry across northern Australia.

Stopping by the Torres Strait Light Infantry and Returned Services League (RSL) memorial, I was proud to honour and reflect on family members and other Torres Strait Islanders who served in World War II. I felt proud to see my great-grandfather Victor Blanco and great-uncle George Ganomi Blanco included on the memorial. Granddad Victor is an important person in Torres Strait Islander history. Also a pearl-shell diver by occupation, he served as a corporal with the 2/31st Battalion, Second Australian Imperial Force (2nd AIF, 7th Division) in the Middle East and North Africa and with the Royal Australian Army Engineers (1st Port Maintenance Company and 2/2nd Australian Docks Operations Company) in New Guinea.

In 2014, I began researching and co-authoring *A Question of Colour* with Mum. We were in Cairns when we spontaneously travelled to Bamaga and Mer via Horn and Thursday Islands. During that trip, we stopped by Granddad Victor's grave at the Old Injinoo Cemetery. We also connected with our oldest living relative at the time, Uncle Rusty Williams, who has since passed away. We were made to feel very welcome by Rusty and his children Reg, Bolly, Fannie, Fred, Ronnie and Michael, and their families. We spent the days discussing our connections and family tree and listening to Uncle Rusty's stories about Grandma Aggie and my second-great-grandmother Annie Blanco. On Thursday Island we also connected with other family members we had not met before. There was an immediate bond.

Going home to Mer was a sacred experience, and flying over the Great Barrier Reef was unforgettable. I remained glued to the plane window, mesmerised by the changing colours of the sea below. Arriving on the island was akin to stepping on hallowed ground, standing on the same soil my ancestors have lived on since time immemorial and seeing the villages in which many generations of my family were born. I will never regret taking that trip and am glad to have had Mum as my companion. It is a moment I continue to cherish and will forever hold dear. I feel more whole in my identity for going to Mer. We've since lost several relatives we met on that visit; this reaffirms the importance of living in the moment and saying yes to opportunities like this when they arise. I have also travelled to the Philippines to research my family history. Ireland and England are next on my bucket list.

Nowadays, I am not alone in seeking my place and belonging as a Torres Strait Islander. Our diaspora is significant, and our histories and experiences are incredibly diverse. From Melbourne and Darwin to Alice Springs, Port Hedland, Karratha, Tom Price and Paraburdoo in the Pilbara region of Western Australia, I have had the privilege of meeting many other Torres Strait Islanders through my work and travels in the mining industry. I enjoy listening to their stories and always feel strengthened by our connections.

We are a thriving, resilient people, and we continue to succeed in our chosen professions, from the arts and music to academia, entertainment, film and television, sports, health, defence, hospitality, education, mining, law and public service. A few years ago in Perth, I met a Murray Islander who served as a highway patrol officer in Fresno, California. I wouldn't have believed it if she hadn't shared photos of herself in uniform. It reminded me that we, as a people, are geographically dispersed.

I am a little envious of other Islanders who had the opportunity to grow up back home, antap (on top) in the Torres Strait, and of those who were raised with ailan kastom (island custom) on the mainland. In many ways, they play an essential role as the custodians and keepers of our culture; they also ensure the continuity of our practices, customs, knowledge and time-honoured traditions. Regardless of where we live and how we were raised, as Torres Strait Islanders we will always remain bound and deeply connected through our ancestral roots and our continued ties to our island home. I get goosebumps and chills whenever I see traditional Torres Strait Islander dancing. It makes me feel so proud to belong to such a unique and vibrant people and culture. Not all Torres Strait Islanders fish, sing, dance, hunt or know our language. But many others do. And, in my case, it's never too late to learn.

# Notes on the Contributors

*Editor*

SAMANTHA FAULKNER is a Torres Strait Islander and Aboriginal woman, from Badu and Moa Islands in the Torres Strait and the Yadhaigana and Wuthathi peoples of Cape York Peninsula, Queensland. She is the proud author of *Life Blong Ali Drummond: A Life in the Torres Strait*, (Aboriginal Studies Press, 2007) and editor of *Pamle: Torres Strait Islanders in Canberra* (2018).

Her poetry and short stories are published nationally and internationally. She is a member of the ACT Aboriginal and Torres Strait Islander Arts Network and MARION (ACT Writers). She is Treasurer, First Nations Australia Writers Network, ACT Torres Strait Islander Corporation and Us Mob Writing Group. She was the inaugural Torres Strait Islander curator for the 2023 Brisbane Writers Festival.

ELLEN ARMSTRONG was born and raised on Awabakal country and has been living in Meanjin for the past nine years. Being of Torres Strait Islander, Japanese and Scottish decent, Ellen's passionate about celebrating all cultures with family, friends and those around her. Ellen's story is dedicated to her great-grandmother and grandmother.

TETEI BAKIC-TAPIM was born in Gimuy and was raised in Dharug Ngurra. Her family is from Mer Island and Erub Island (Torres Strait Islands), Bindal, Kaanju and Juru (Queensland), Gaire Village and Korobosea Village (Central Province, Papua New Guinea) and Bečej (Serbia). Tetei works in the Department of Indigenous Studies, Wallumattagal Campus (Macquarie University) as the Department Coordinator and is also completing a Master of Research as a pathway to a PhD. She is passionate about archiving her grandparents' stories advocating for Torres Strait Islanders living on the mainland. Her chapter in this book would not be possible without the many hours she spent on the phone with her grandparents going over all the details and naming the many families involved in the history of Magani Malu Kes. Her chapter is dedicated to her niece, Ama, so she can read about her great-grandparents and the future they envisioned for her.

JIMI BANI is an award-winning actor for stage, film and television. He graduated from Western Australian Academy of Performing Arts in 2007. His television and film credits include the 2012 film *Mabo*, directed by Rachel Perkins, in which he played the titular role, as well as regular roles on *RAN: Remote Area Nurse* (SBS), *Black Snow* (Stan Original), *The Straits* (ABC),

*Redfern Now* (ABC) and *Black Comedy* (ABC), among others. Jimi's stage credits include lead roles for national theatres, and in 2021 he won the Matilda Award for Best Leading Actor in *Who's Afraid of Virginia Woolf?*, State Theatre Company of South Australia and Queensland Theatre. In 2023, Jimi starred in the solo show *Every Brilliant Thing* with the State Theatre Company of South Australia.

LEILANI BIN-JUDA joined the Australian public service in 1995 and served in a variety of roles, both in Australia and overseas, working on key international operations and whole of government initiatives. She is deeply committed to improving the social, cultural, environmental and economic development of Indigenous Australians. In 2019, she was awarded a Public Service Medal for promoting Indigenous heritage in Australia's cultural and foreign policies. Ms Bin-Juda is an active proponent of championing women in leadership and mentoring. In 2020, she was appointed as the first substantive female CEO for the Torres Strait Regional Authority. In 2022, she rejoined the Department of Foreign Affairs and Trade to undertake overseas assignments, and was appointed as Australia's High Commissioner to the Federal Republic of Nigeria in 2023.

TAHLIA BOWIE is a Torres Strait Islander, raised on both Hammond Island and Thursday Island. Her family is from Kulkalgal and Maluilgal nations. She is a fashion designer and co-owner of clothing label Bowie Empire, which incorporates Torres Strait Islander emblems into high-end streetwear. Her business has been recognised by *GQ* magazine and showcased at the *Deadly Threads* exhibition at the State Library of Queensland and the Cairns Art Gallery.

JILLIAN BOYD-BOWIE is a Zenadth Kes woman from the Samsep and Zagareb tribes of Erub and Mer. Jillian is a mother, grandmother, published author, poet, mentor and businesswoman who invests her craft and creativity to inspire and empower First Nation peoples and inform a listening wider audience.

AALIYAH-JADE BRADBURY is a proud Indigenous woman from the Larrakia Nation of Garramilla (Darwin) and Erubam Le peoples of Meriam Mir, and an Emmy-nominated storyteller. Aaliyah-Jade is most well known for producing the film *Harley & Katya* (2022). She has been recognised by Screen Australia and Screen NSW as 'one to watch' for the way she highlights intricate storytelling through the humanity of our First Nations peoples. She has also held various roles in NGOs and government at organisations such as Creative Australia (formerly the Australia Council for the Arts), the ABC and SBS.

JOHN DOOLAH is a Meriam-Samsep man. His mother is Zeub-Komet. He completed his schooling on mainland Australia and worked on the railways with his father before embarking on a new career path. He enrolled at university and graduated with a double degree, master's degree and PhD. John has been a respected lecturer at University of Newcastle and the University of Melbourne, where he was Lecturer in Indigenous Education (2021–2023) at the Melbourne Graduate School of Education (now Faculty of Education). He is currently a Ngarrngga Postdoctral Fellow at the University of Melbourne.

DONISHA DUFF OAM is an Aboriginal and Torres Strait Islander woman from Thursday Island in the Torres Strait. She has familial links with Moa, Badu and Mabuiag Islands (Torres Strait) and is a Yadhaigana/Wuthathi Aboriginal traditional owner (Cape York).

She has over twenty-years' experience in health policy, planning and management with a particular focus on Aboriginal and Torres Strait Islander health and preventative health. Donisha has worked at various levels of Federal and State government, and the non-government sector, including as ministerial policy adviser to Warren Snowdon MP, former Minister for Indigenous Health.

Donisha is an Adjunct Associate Professor at Edith Cowen University (WA) and has a Bachelor of Arts (Hons) from Griffith University and a Masters of Business Administration (MBA) from the Australian National University. She was awarded National NAIDOC Scholar of the Year 2014. She is a Churchill Fellow (2015). She was awarded the Medal of the Order of Australia in 2024.

AARON FA'AOSO is a Torres Strait Islander actor and film producer. He is co-chair of the Queensland government's Interim Truth and Treaty Body. He serves on the board of SBS, as well as the boards of Screen Queensland and Supply Nation. His screen credits include *Strait to the Plate*, *Blue Water Empire*, *Black Comedy*, *The Straits*, *RAN: Remote Area Nurse* and *East West 101*. He co-wrote his memoir, *So Far, So Good* (Pantera Publishing, 2022) with MICHELLE SCOTT TUCKER. Michelle is also the author of *Elizabeth Macarthur: A Life at the Edge of the World* (Text Publishing, 2018).

ELLIE GAFFNEY (1932–2007) grew up on Thursday Island and Cape York Peninsula. She trained as a nurse and worked in various hospitals in Brisbane, Darwin and Thursday Island. When, despite her better qualification, a white male nurse got a job instead of her, she gave up her nursing career and became a campaigner and advocate for improving Torres Strait Islander conditions. Ellie was a founding member of the Mura Kosker Sorority, the Torres Strait Islander Media Association and Star of the Sea Home for the Aged. Her books include *Somebody Now* (Aboriginal Studies Press, 1989) and *Mura Solwata Kosher: We Saltwater Women* (Verdant House, 2007), and her autobiographical essay 'Determination to Succeed' was published in *In Our Own Right: Black Australian Nurses' Stories* (Routledge, 2005). She was awarded the Order of Australia medal in 1990 in recognition of her service to the community.

VELMA GARA's family is from the Torres Strait, the Eastern Islands of Erub and Mer. Her father has family connection to Kubin Village. Her totems are Serar (bird) and Beizam (shark). Velma is a freelance journalist and broadcaster/producer and has played basketball in local, state and international competitions. She has worked in the media industry, in radio, television news and print, for forty years.

JAQUI HUGHES is ipeka of Wagadagam (Mabuyag Island) of Zenadh. She has beautiful strong sisters and lives on Larrakia Country, with her husband and two sons, and is still learning wise ways to live from her mother and mother's family and father and father's family. These knowledges add value to her other roles as a doctor, advocate and health entrepreneur (as a clinician, researcher, mentor and teacher). Stand in your power, young ones. You are deeply loved and loveable.

ADAM C. LEES is a mining and resources expert, specialising in community relations and sustainability since 2000. Hailing from Mount Isa, he was educated at Monash University, Queensland University of Technology and Griffith University. With wanderlust and a zeal for photography, he has explored over sixty countries, residing and working in six.

DR RHETT LOBAN is a Torres Strait Islander with connections to Mabuyag and Boigu. Rhett is a researcher and lecturer at Macquarie University. His research interests include culture, game-based learning and virtual reality.

THOMAS LOWAH (1914–1989) was a pearler, activist and writer, whose autobiography was one of the first ever published by a Torres Strait Islander author. He worked as a diver on pearling luggers, sailing the waters of the Torres Strait and the Great Barrier Reef, and he served as a Corporal with the Torres Strait Islander Infantry Battalion during World War II. Beyond his formidable experiences, Thomas emerged as a committed leader and a resounding voice advocating for the rights of Torres Strait Islander people. He played a pivotal role as one of the architects in championing the cause for fair compensation owed to Torres Strait Islander ex-servicemen, navigating the complexities and paving the way for their rightful restitution. His dedication for justice echoes his unwavering commitment to his community's welfare. We were unable to source a childhood photo of him.

EDWARD KOIKI MABO (1936–1992) was a Torres Strait Islander community leader and land rights campaigner born on Mer, in the Murray group of islands. He is known for his pivotal role in the landmark High Court cases *Mabo v Queensland*, which overturned the concept of terra nullius and recognised native title land rights. His biography was written with his friend of twenty-five years, Professor NOEL LOOS (University of Queensland Press, 1996).

THOMAS MAYO is a Kaurareg Aboriginal and Kalkalgal, Erubamle Torres Strait Islander man. He is the Assistant National Secretary of the Maritime Union of Australia. Thomas is a signatory of the *Uluru Statement from the Heart* and has been a leading advocate since its inception in May 2017. He is the Chairperson of the Northern Territory Indigenous Labor Network and a director on the Australians for Indigenous Constitutional Recognition board. Thomas is the author of six books, including the bestselling *The Voice to Parliament Handbook: All The Details You Need* with eminent journalist Kerry O'Brien (Hardie Grant, 2023).

LENORA THAKER descends from Erub and Mabuyag Islands and lives on Gimuy Walubara Yidinji country. She is a published writer and was awarded the 2021 Boundless Indigenous Writers Prize for her forthcoming historical novel about a family of Torres Strait Islanders living on a mainland shantytown around World War II.

SORREN THOMAS is a Mualgul woman of Moa Island who was born and raised on Darumbal Country, Rockhampton, Queensland. She is currently living in Naarm working at the Royal Melbourne Hospital, having completed her Doctor of Medicine at the University of Notre Dame, Sydney, in 2023, and previously completed her Bachelor of Biomedical Science at Bond University in 2019. Sorren is a proud advocate for Indigenous health and cultural awareness, was the inaugural Indigenous

Representative for her medical student society. She hopes to work in the field of Indigenous eye health throughout our Aboriginal and Torres Strait Islander communities.

INA TITASEY (1927–2014) was born on Naghir Island in the Torres Strait, and grew up surrounded by nature and colour as she fished, gardened and played with her siblings and cousins. She spent her later childhood at a Catholic convent on Thursday Island, where she and her sister Cessa were 'trapped like the pigs' and always under the watchful eyes of the nuns. In her later life, she travelled the world as part of The Mills Sisters singing group, which won a Red Orche Award in 1995. Ina's story is recorded by her daughter-in-law, CATHERINE TITASEY. Catherine was married to Ina's son Tony, with whom she has four children. She lived on Thursday Island for twenty years and now lives on the mainland and works as a special education teacher. She is also the author of the crime novel *My Island Homicide* (University of Queensland Press, 2012).

LOCKEAH WAPAU was born and raised in Mackay, Queensland. His parents are Frank and Denise Wapau, and he has one brother, Juliean. Lockeah has lived in Shepparton, Victoria, for the last nineteen years with his son, Noah Wapau, and currently works in the rail industry as a track inspector.

DANIELLA WILLIAMS is a proud Indigenous woman from Thursday Island, Torres Strait. She is both Aboriginal and Torres Strait Islander, mixed with Malaysian bloodlines. At home, she speaks Torres Strait Creole, and English is her second language. Through songs and storytelling, she tries her best to preserve our language.

# Real people.
# Real stories.

Discover the bestselling Growing Up series

### Growing Up Asian in Australia
Edited by Alice Pung

Asian-Australians have often been written about by outsiders, as outsiders. In this collection, compiled by award-winning author Alice Pung, they tell their own stories with verve, courage and a large dose of humour.

### Growing Up Aboriginal in Australia
Edited by Anita Heiss

*Winner – Small Publishers' Adult Book of the Year, Australian Book Industry Awards 2019*

What is it like to grow up Aboriginal in Australia? This anthology, compiled by award-winning author Anita Heiss, show-cases diverse voices, experiences and stories to answer that question. Each account reveals, to some degree, the impacts of invasion and colonisation – on language, on Country, on ways of life, and on how people are treated daily in the community, the education system, the workplace and friendship groups.

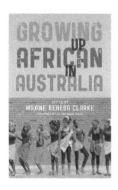

### Growing Up African in Australia
Edited by Maxine Beneba Clarke with Ahmed Yussuf and Magan Magan

Compiled by award-winning author Maxine Beneba Clarke, with curatorial assistance from writers Ahmed Yussuf and Magan Magan, this anthology brings together voices from the regions of Africa and the African diaspora, including the Caribbean and the Americas. Told with passion, power and poise, these are the stories of African-diaspora Australians.

### Growing Up Queer in Australia
Edited by Benjamin Law

*'For better or worse, sooner or later, life conspires to reveal you to yourself, and this is growing up.'*

Compiled by celebrated author and journalist Benjamin Law, *Growing Up Queer in Australia* assembles voices from across the spectrum of LGBTIQA+ identity. Spanning diverse places, eras, ethnicities and experiences, these are the stories of growing up queer in Australia.

### Growing Up Disabled in Australia
Edited by Carly Findlay

One in five Australians has a disability. And disability presents itself in many ways. Yet disabled people are still under-represented in the media and in literature. In *Growing Up Disabled in Australia* – compiled by writer and appearance activist Carly Findlay OAM – more than forty writers with a disability or chronic illness share their stories, in their own words. The result is illuminating.

### Growing Up in Australia
Edited by Black Inc.

Featuring pieces from across the Growing Up series and gems from essential Australian memoirs such as Rick Morton's *100 Years of Dirt* and Magda Szubanski's *Reckoning, Growing Up in Australia* captures the diversity of our nation in moving and revelatory ways.

### Growing Up in Country Australia
Edited by Rick Morton

A fresh, modern look at country Australia, with stories of joy, adventure, nostalgia, connection to nature and freedom, but also more grim tales – of drought, fires, mouse plagues and isolation. Across nearly forty stories by established and emerging authors, *Growing Up in Country Australia* captures a unique and revealing snapshot of rural life.

### Growing Up Torres Strait Islander in Australia
Edited by Samantha Faulkner

*Growing Up Torres Strait Islander in Australia* showcases the distinct identity of Torres Strait Islanders through their diverse voices and journeys. Hear from emerging and established writers from both today and the recent past as they share their joy, culture, good eating, lessons learned and love of family, language and Country.

### Growing Up Indian in Australia
Edited by Aarti Betigeri

'Indian-Australian' is not a one-size-fits-all descriptor. Given the depth and richness of diversity of the Indian subcontinent, it is fitting that its diaspora is similarly varied. This colourful, energetic anthology offers reflections on identity, culture, family, food and expectations, ultimately revealing deep truths about both Australian and Indian life.

## Explore the series
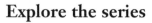
blackincbooks.com.au/series/growing-series

Milton Keynes UK
Ingram Content Group UK Ltd.
UKHW011132220424
441551UK00006B/487

9 781760 644420